T0120790

# SAVED
# AND SURE,
# SAFE
# AND SECURE

## THE ETERNAL SECURITY
## OF THE BELIEVER

JOHN DAVID MARTIN

WESTBOW
PRESS®
A DIVISION OF THOMAS NELSON
& ZONDERVAN

This book is a work of non-fiction. Unless otherwise noted, the author and the publisher make no explicit guarantees as to the accuracy of the information contained in this book and in some cases, names of people and places have been altered to protect their privacy.

WestBow Press books may be ordered through booksellers or by contacting:

WestBow Press
A Division of Thomas Nelson & Zondervan
1663 Liberty Drive
Bloomington, IN 47403
www.westbowpress.com
844-714-3454

Because of the dynamic nature of the Internet, any web addresses or links contained in this book may have changed since publication and may no longer be valid. The views expressed in this work are solely those of the author and do not necessarily reflect the views of the publisher, and the publisher hereby disclaims any responsibility for them.

Any people depicted in stock imagery provided by Getty Images are models, and such images are being used for illustrative purposes only. Certain stock imagery © Getty Images.

All Scripture quotations are taken from the King James Version.

ISBN: 978-1-6642-0216-0 (sc)
ISBN: 978-1-6642-0217-7 (hc)
ISBN: 978-1-6642-0215-3 (e)

Library of Congress Control Number: 2020915607

Print information available on the last page.

WestBow Press rev. date: 02/05/2024

**Disclaimer:** I prefer and use the "old" King James Version (KJV) of the Holy Scriptures in all my preaching, teaching, and writing. My personal conviction is that the King James Version is the inspired and preserved word of God. As such, I believe that it is still the best available translation of the Bible in the English language for Bible study, memorization, and publicly proclaiming the word of God with power and authority. Any deviation from the KJV is unintentional.

The KJV uses italics where words have been added by the translators to smooth out the English translation from the underlying original Greek and Hebrew texts; *where italics are used in my Scripture citations throughout this work, they are not the KJV italics, but mine for emphasis in this work.*

Let it be noted that truth is truth, wherever it is found or whomever says it. Some of the sources cited are by writers who may not hold to my convictions or beliefs or opinions on certain issues, and citing them in this work is not an endorsement for any false teachings or unscriptural positions they may take.

**Author's Credentials:** The author attended Pensacola Bible Institute, where he earned his Bachelor of Divinity degree, graduating in 1984. He was ordained to the Gospel Ministry on January 1, 1986. In 2008, the author received his Master of Biblical Studies degree from Gulf Coast Baptist Bible Institute & Seminary in Fort Walton Beach, Florida. David has been in his current pastorate at Solid Rock Baptist Church in Bartlett, Tennessee, since 2002.

# CONTENTS

# INTRODUCTION

This study will examine what the scriptures have to say about the eternal security of the believer. Just what is "eternal security"? It is the teaching that when a person comes to Jesus Christ for salvation and receives Him by faith as their personal Savior, God forgives them of all their sins (past, present, and future)—and from that point onward they are "SAVED FOREVER." Ankerberg and Weldon state that God's born-again children "possess eternal life at the instant we place our trust in Jesus Christ. Eternal life began at the moment of saving faith and *continues forever* throughout eternity."[1] Dr. Charles C. Ryrie, well-known author and longtime professor of systematic theology at Dallas Theological Seminary, proposed this definition: "Eternal security is that work of God which guarantees that the gift of salvation, once received, is possessed forever and cannot be lost."[2] The founder of what is today Dallas Theological Seminary, Dr. Lewis Sperry Chafer, wrote that "there is no Scripture, when rightly divided and related to the whole testimony of God, that teaches that a Christian may be lost. Nor is there any example in the Bible."[3] I wholeheartedly agree.

Unfortunately, controversy surrounds this particular doctrine. The question of whether a Christian, that is a born-again believer, can lose their salvation, has been debated for centuries. There is much strong disagreement among good men and women of faith on this topic. The answer to the question "Can a person who has trusted Jesus Christ as personal Savior, once saved, be lost again?" is either yes or no. Dr. Chafer says, "There is no middle position; both answers cannot be true at the same time." Either a person is saved or lost; and if saved, a Christian is either eternally secure or not.

At the outset, we ought to distinguish between salvation, eternal security, and the assurance of salvation. Salvation is obtained by receiving Christ as Savior (John 1:12) and trusting in His redemptive work on the Cross in our behalf to freely forgive us our sins and freely give us eternal life (Romans 5:8; Romans 6:23). Assurance of salvation is the personal confidence a believer has in knowing that they are saved, forgiven, justified, redeemed, and so on (i.e., simply put, we know we are saved and going to heaven when we die, because of what Jesus did for us on the Cross and in our hearts [1 John 5:10–13]). But eternal security is the teaching that Christians are "once saved, always saved." And even if a truly saved person doesn't accept that doctrine, if it is true (which we have no doubt about), then it doesn't matter what you think or how you feel; the fact is that if you've trusted Christ as Savior, you were saved at that moment, you've been saved ever since, you're saved now, and you will be saved in the future and on into eternity. What a blessing that is! As Fanny Crosby said it in song: "Blessed assurance, Jesus is mine; Oh, what a foretaste of glory divine!"

Among the criticisms those of the Baptist faith receive, probably no doctrine held by our faith tradition is called into question more than our staunch belief in the eternal security of the believer. It has been called a *"blessed* doctrine" by men like Charles Spurgeon and an *"accursed* doctrine" by men like Jimmy Swaggart (equating the teaching of "once saved, always saved" [OSAS] with a perversion of the Gospel, by misapplying the apostle Paul's condemnation of a false gospel in Galatians 1:8, 9, and alluding to Simon Peter's censure of heresies in 2 Peter 2:1 as "damnable," as translated in the King James Version).

The Roman Catholic Church in essence calls it the "sin of *presumption."* According to the Catholic Encyclopedia, "Presumption is here considered as a vice. ... It may also be regarded as a product of pride. It may be defined as the condition of a soul which, because of a badly regulated reliance on God's mercy and power, hopes for salvation without doing anything to deserve it."⁴ In their system, to state it plainly, they teach that you are anathema and will go to hell for believing that you can know you are saved. To one Roman Catholic apologist,

> Salvation is not guaranteed. ... Many fundamentalist denominations profess that Christ actually promised that Heaven is theirs in exchange for a remarkably simple act; they are only required at one point in their lives, to 'accept Jesus as their personal Savior.' ... living well is not crucial and it does not affect their salvation. ... Christ has redeemed us, but this is not a guarantee of salvation; it is just a necessary prelude. Jesus did His part, now we have to do ours. ... Fundamentalist teaching is that God 'covers' our sins so we can be saved, even with those sins on our souls. In his booklet called *There*

*is Therefore Now No Condemnation*, Wilson Erwin writes: ' ... the person who places his faith in Jesus Christ and His Blood shed at Calvary is eternally secure. He can never lose his salvation.' This is the purest form of fundamentalist teaching, but is in direct confrontation with the teaching of the ... Catholic Church!"[5]

Evangelical Christians who deny the doctrine of eternal security, most of whom reject Roman Catholicism, find themselves in agreement with the Catholic Church on this point. This statement by an evangelical Mennonite writer is typical: "Nowhere does the Bible suggest that a person who one time believed in Christ is ... assured of final salvation."[6]

Those who accept the teaching of eternal security, and believe the Scriptures clearly teach it, have been maligned as people who promote a careless lifestyle and imply that Christians have a "license to sin" because they believe in "once saved, always saved." The nineteenth century American evangelist Charles G. Finney said that "if this doctrine inspires any man to commit sin, it only shows that he never did repent; he only pretended to repent."[7] Those who reject the doctrine of eternal security believe that a Christian can "lose their salvation" through careless living. Some call it *conditional* eternal security,[8] which is no security at all.

Proponents of eternal security have typically been referred to as *Calvinists* and its opponents called *Arminians*. This goes back to the Council of Dort in 1609. According to the accepted definitions, the Calvinist believes in salvation by grace and "once saved, always saved," whereas the Arminian believes in salvation by grace but that one can "fall from grace" and "lose salvation" if one does not live right. The Calvinist believes "saved by grace, kept by faith." The Arminian believes "saved by grace, kept by faith *and works.*"

The doctrine of eternal security is one of the five particular tenets Baptists embrace that mark them as Baptists, known as the "Baptist distinctives," the other four being the absolute separation of church and state; believer's baptism (by immersion); a regenerated church membership; and the priesthood of the believer. [It should be mentioned that among the Baptists there is one group that rejects eternal security and believes that a Christian can "lose" their salvation, and that is the Freewill Baptists.]

Just because a person is a member of a Baptist church does not mean they are truly a Baptist or saved. In too many Baptist churches, there are those who neither understand nor believe in eternal security, which makes them *not* Baptists *nor* Bible-believing Christians. An example of the ignorance and the pitiful condition of many Baptist churches is illustrated by the following incident.

A friend was attending a Southern Baptist Sunday school in Memphis, Tennessee. One morning, the topic of discussion was false prophets, and the teacher asked the class to give some examples of false prophets. My friend raised his hand, the teacher called on him, and he said that Jimmy Swaggart was a false prophet.

A long-time member of the class took offense and blurted out, "Why!"

My friend answered, "Because he doesn't believe in eternal security."

The man asked, "What's *that?*"

My friend showed him scripture and explained it to him.

The man replied, "That's *your* interpretation."

Sad to say, that man is typical of many so-called Baptists.

So, how is it that so many professing Christians, even Baptists, can be so confused and ignorant about a basic Bible doctrine? The answer is that either the church's leaders are not properly teaching the Bible or the members are unsaved or unspiritual and therefore have no biblical discernment, or both. Such members fall prey to the cultists and heretics and may eventually subscribe to their false teachings, one of them being the denial of eternal security. False prophets are considered Bible-denying heretics because they not only *disagree* with what the Bible teaches, but they actually *deny* what the Bible says.

Dr. Charles Stanley has written on the idea of a Christian "losing salvation" or forfeiting eternal life: "In the case of salvation God has a strict no-return policy. There is no evidence by way of statement or illustration that God has ever taken back from a believer the gift of salvation once it has been given."[9]

The teaching that denies eternal security, as any false doctrine, is arrived at by "privately interpreting" the Scriptures (2 Peter 1:20). The reason for false conclusions and heretical teachings is either due to misunderstanding, misinterpreting, or misapplying the Scriptures, or a combination thereof.

As a general rule, the serious Bible student must understand the Bible in view of complete statements instead of incomplete ones. To properly interpret the Bible on any given subject, one must examine any seemingly unclear, difficult-to-understand verse in the light of ten other clear verses about which there is no misunderstanding. The heretic will do the opposite—he or she will interpret ten clear verses in view of his group's one, favorite obscure verse in order to build a false doctrine upon. For instance, the so-called "Church of Christ" will interpret all verses on baptism in view of Acts 2:38 instead of the other way around and falsely conclude that water baptism is a prerequisite condition for receiving the forgiveness of sins; they make baptism a sacrament rather than an ordinance of the church. (Just to be clear: any group, sect, denomination, or cult that teaches water baptism is necessary for the forgiveness of sins is promoting a false doctrine that will mislead lost souls to hell.)

Heretics also mistake the literal for the figurative and the figurative for the literal. For examples, (1) the *Roman Catholic Church* takes John 6 literally, thus fallaciously enforcing their teaching of the Mass, that the elements used in their perversion of the biblical Lord's Supper become the literal body and blood of Christ to be received at the hands of the priest and swallowed and digested physically (this is how the Roman Catholic understands "receiving Christ") and (2) the *Protestants* take Revelation 20 figuratively, and thus rule out the literal thousand-year reign of Christ on this earth during the period known as *the Millennium*, replacing it with the metaphorical struggle of good versus evil.

It's admitted that among genuine Christians there are honest disagreements over Bible doctrines, but among true believers there are essential Christian doctrines that all will universally hold to without much distinction. The fundamental teachings about the virgin birth, the deity of Christ, the resurrection of Christ, justification by faith, and the inerrancy of the Bible are all going to be commonly held beliefs by Christians. But there are some doctrines that many good Christians debate and disagree about that are not considered to be necessary Christian truths. In other words, you can disagree on them and still be a Christian. Some of those would be teachings concerning the details of the Second Coming of Christ, such as when the Rapture will occur and whether the Bible teaches premillennialism, postmillennialism or a-millennialism. The doctrine of eternal security falls into this category. It isn't essential to believe it to be saved, but if you are saved, you'll most likely see the truth of it from the Scriptures.

More to the point of this present study on eternal security is the difference between what theologians classify as *Calvinists* (those who affirm the doctrine of eternal security) and *Arminians* (those who deny the doctrine of eternal security). Both the Calvinist and the Arminian are firmly convinced that they are right. When looking at a Christian apostatizing (i.e., backsliding, going off into sin, and so on), the Calvinist and Arminian perspectives are as follows: The Calvinist says the Christian did not lose salvation, but that they never were saved to begin with and need to *"really* get saved." The Arminian says the Christian lost their salvation and needs to get saved *again*! Hence, some churches have what are known as "retreads." The doctrine of Calvinism called the perseverance of the saints is not as some think—eternal security—but actually, it's the idea that if you're truly saved you won't apostatize; if you do, then you need to *really* get saved. This leads to the recycling of church members getting saved two and three and four times in their lifetimes, when in fact they probably were really saved but had doubt placed into their minds by preaching that says that *if* you are *really* saved, you *won't* do this or that and so on.

When it comes to Bible study, theology, and religious discussion, it would be wise to remember the words of the

Quaker founder of Pennsylvania, William Penn, who said, "Neither despise nor oppose what thou dost not understand."[10] The apostle Paul admonishes his audience to "prove all things" and then to "hold fast that which is good" (1 Thessalonians 5:21). The Bereans were commended because "they searched the scriptures daily" to see "whether those things" that Paul preached and taught "were so" (Acts 17:11).

For those who aren't familiar with or haven't been exposed to a clear presentation of the doctrine of eternal security, I believe they will find this study most interesting and, I trust, a real blessing to their souls.

In the following pages, the object of this thesis will be to analyze the biblical truths that teach and reinforce the certainty of eternal security: the scriptural fact that once a person repents of their sins and receives the Lord Jesus Christ as their personal Savior, they are forever saved. It's my contention that all who call on the name of the Lord (Romans 10:13) may be saved and sure, safe and secure.

# SAVED BY THE GRACE OF GOD

*For by grace are ye saved through faith; and that not of yourselves: it is the gift of God: Not of works, lest any man should boast. For we are his workmanship, created in Christ Jesus unto good works, which God hath before ordained that we should walk in them.*

—EPHESIANS 2:8–10

The above scripture is one of the most well-known and beloved passages in the Bible to the born-again child of God. It expresses the truth of salvation by grace. Paul the apostle even called this the message of salvation; he preached "the gospel of the grace of God" (Acts 20:24).

One of the problems that led some to reject the doctrine of eternal security is misunderstanding the very doctrine of salvation itself. Wherever there is confusion concerning how a person *attains* salvation, there's going to be confusion concerning how one *maintains* that salvation.

What is salvation, and what does it mean to be saved? In a nutshell, it means that God *forgives you of your sins* so you do not have to go to hell (Acts 10:43, 13:38–39; Colossians 1:14; Romans 6:23a) and *gives you eternal life* so you can go to heaven (Romans 6:23b; 1 John 5:13). In addition to that, you become a new creature in Christ (2 Corinthians 5:17), and the Lord Himself comes into your heart to live (Colossians 1:27). The Lord will be with you in this life, and you will be with Him in the next.

Ephesians 2:8–10 clearly reveals the way of salvation. It tells how God saves a sinner. And the topic of discussion, the doctrine of eternal security, is inherently taught in these verses as well.

## THE METHOD OF SALVATION

The Bible plainly declares the method of salvation in verse 8: "For *by grace* are ye saved."

Because God is a good God, a compassionate God, a loving God, a merciful God, and a gracious God, the salvation of God can only be by grace. Humanity can be saved because God's mercy endures forever and His compassions fail not (Psalm 136; Lamentations 3:22).

The grace of God "came by Jesus Christ" (John 1:17) who was "full of grace" (John 1:14) and has "appeared to all men" (Titus 2:11) and is offered to all men. In Him, those saved by grace "have redemption through his blood, the forgiveness of sins, according to the riches of his grace" (Ephesians 1:7).

*Grace* is defined as "the unmerited, unearned, undeserved favor of God that He bestows on believing sinners." Salvation by grace means salvation that is free, gratis, for nothing, without cost. Salvation through the imputed righteousness of Christ is a gift by grace, which is a free gift according to the apostle Paul (Romans 5:15, 16, 18).

There is no disputing the fact that salvation is by grace, and by extension, none should dispute the inherent truth of eternal security by grace as well. The principles of grace include the keeping power of God unto salvation (1 Peter 1:5); they imply God's keeping power in that the Lord has decreed that the elect shall be saved (Romans 5:9, 10; 10:13); and the keeping power of God is indicated by the manifold provisions and safeguards, which the Lord has made to that end. "Should the eternal purpose of God fail by the slightest degree, the object of salvation, the object of the death and resurrection of Christ, and the object of creation itself, will have failed."[11] We can be certain that the all-powerful God of creation and redemption will not lose one soul who has placed the keeping of their soul into His care, "being confident of this very thing, that he which hath begun a good work in you will perform it until the day of Jesus Christ" (Philippians 1:6).

We repeat the old adage that if one cannot be saved by their (good) works, then neither can they be lost again because of (bad) works. Salvation cannot be *merited* nor *demerited*. Human ability has no part in *getting* saved or *staying* saved. Charles Spurgeon, speaking of genuine Christianity, explained that "true religion is supernatural at its beginning, supernatural in its continuance, and supernatural in its close. It is the work of God from first to last."[12] Dr. Chafer said, "As certainly as grace is the one and only basis upon which God can save a meritless sinner, so certainly grace alone is the basis upon which God can righteously keep him saved."[13] Salvation is wholly by grace, from start to finish.

We can all agree that no one is good enough or righteous

enough or meritorious enough to *attain* salvation based upon good works. By the same token, it only seems logical that no one is good enough or righteous enough or meritorious enough to *maintain* salvation based upon his or her own good works. The Christian is *saved* by grace and *kept* saved by grace.

## THE MISTAKE OF SALVATION

The Bible plainly declares the mistake concerning salvation in Ephesians 2:8–9: "For by grace are ye saved through faith; and that *not of yourselves: it is the gift of God: not of works*, lest any man should boast."

Most people make the mistake of believing that salvation is ultimately up to them, based upon their own good works. But the Bible plainly states in these verses that salvation is not up to humans and not based upon works.

In no uncertain terms, the Bible says that if salvation is by grace, then it's no more of works (Romans 11:6). The Bible is very clear on this point—that salvation is "not by works of righteousness which we have done, but according to his mercy he saved us" (Titus 3:5). Our works can't save us, for even the best we could possibly do isn't good enough! Why? Because "all our righteousnesses are as filthy rags" in the sight of God (Isaiah 64:6).

How much plainer can the Bible be? According to Paul in Romans 4:16, salvation "is of faith, that it might be by grace."

In the same chapter, the Bible says, "Now to him that worketh is the reward *not* reckoned of grace, but of *debt*" (Romans 4:4). In plainer words, if salvation could be earned by good works, then God would owe salvation to the sinner who did the best they could. But a true child of God does not "frustrate the grace of God" (Galatians 2:21). Genuine Christians understand that if living right and keeping the law could save their souls, then Jesus Christ's death on the Cross was all for naught (in vain). As one Christian bumper sticker asks, "If you can earn it, why did Jesus die?" If salvation were of works, and not of grace, then all humankind would be lost forever without any hope of heaven.

It must be understood that grace and works are antithetical concepts in the scheme of God's redemptive plan. They are mutually exclusive of each other. Those who teach that believing is a work required for salvation will have to explain away Romans 4:5, where Paul clearly says that the act of believing is *not* working for salvation. One could go so far as to say, according to what Paul wrote in Ephesians 2:8 and Galatians 2:16, that it is not even the Christian's faith really but *Christ's faith given to the believing sinner* and exercised in Him, that brings final salvation in the end (see 1 Peter 1:9). It really *is* all of grace.

In spite of these clear Bible verses and this plain doctrinal teaching, most people will do their best to try and work their way to heaven and earn the favor of God and hope to make it to heaven when they die. And still they are not sure they will make the grade, pass the test, move to the head of the class, and graduate to heaven. They put on airs of being ever so humble so as not to offend God by claiming they are certain of heaven and assured of salvation, yet in essence what they hope to do is stand before God and brag about their goodness, making themselves seemingly deserving of heaven. They will be sadly and shockingly disappointed when they discover that no man struts in the presence of God, for the Bible plainly says in Ephesians 2:9 that salvation is "not of works, lest any man should boast."

## THE MEDIUM OF SALVATION

The Bible plainly declares the medium of salvation in verse 8: "For by grace are ye saved *through faith.*"

Faith is the medium, or channel, through which the grace of God enters the soul and saves the believer. A lost sinner makes contact, so to speak, with God by faith—through believing His Word, the Holy Bible, and acting upon it by receiving Jesus Christ as personal Savior.

Charles G. Finney said that "justification is by faith. Faith is the medium by which the blessing is conveyed to the believer ... It is obvious that if men are saved at all, they must be justified in this way [by faith] and not by the works of the law (Galatians 2:16). ... They are justified by faith, as the medium or instrument. ... Faith is the instrument of our justification. ... You have no right to believe that you will be saved until you have exercised justifying or saving faith [in Christ and His blood atonement]. ... Nothing is justifying faith except believing the testimony that God has given of His Son (1 John 5:10). ... Justifying faith fastens on Christ, takes hold of His atonement, and embraces Him as the only ground of pardon and salvation. ... The gracious pardon will be delivered as soon as you, by one act of faith, receive Jesus Christ as He is offered in the Gospel. ... God never changes His mind once He undertakes the salvation of a soul (Romans 11:29)."[14]

Charles Spurgeon wrote: "Faith occupies the position of a *channel or conduit pipe.* Grace is the fountain and the stream;

6

faith is the aqueduct along which the flood of mercy flows down to refresh the thirsty sons of men."[15] Faith is the "channel of salvation" that links man with God. "Faith saves us because it … brings us into connection with Him."[16] For this reason, therefore, "when a man trusts to his works, or to his sacraments, or to anything of that sort, he will not be saved, because there is no junction between him and Christ."[17] Although people are saved by faith, it isn't faith by itself that saves a person. Dr. Charles Ryrie points out: "The New Testament always says that salvation is *through* faith, not *because* of faith (Ephesians 2:8). Faith is the channel through which we receive God's gift of forgiveness and eternal life."[18] According to E. M. Bounds, commenting on Luke 7:50, "God, through the faith of the sinner, saves him, faith being only the *instrument* that brings salvation to him."[19] To sum up, personal faith is the means by which the saving work of Christ is applied to the one who believes the Gospel message. Biblical salvation comes to the individual believer when they place their complete trust in Christ and His death on the Cross for their sins, believing that Jesus paid all their sin debt with His blood shed on Calvary.

[Charles Stanley draws from an article entitled "The Concept of Faith in the Fourth Gospel," written by Gerald F. Hawthorne and published in *Bibliotheca Sacra*, dated April 1959. He says it is interesting to note the "grammatical construction that occurs repeatedly when faith is mentioned in connection with forgiveness and salvation … The combination of the term for 'believe' and this little preposition ('on' or 'in') is unique to the New Testament … the writers of the New Testament were forced to coin a new phrase to accurately communicate their unique message" of salvation "through faith" by placing one's hope, trust and confidence completely "in" and "upon" the Lord Jesus Christ for their eternal destiny.[20] Charles Ryrie makes an interesting distinction between the prepositions "in" and "on" used in conjunction with believing: (1) to believe "in" Christ indicates our reliance or confidence of trust in the *object of faith*, and (2) to believe "upon" Christ emphasizes the "laying hold" of the *object of faith*. And to be clear, the *object* of faith here meant is the Lord Jesus Christ himself.][21]

Remember the woman who was healed when she touched the hem of Jesus's garment? She is a wonderful illustration of salvation by grace through faith. In Luke 8:42–48 is the story of where "the people thronged" Jesus as He was going to Jairus's house to heal his young daughter. Along the way,

> A woman having an issue of blood twelve years, which had spent all her living upon physicians, neither could be healed of any, Came behind him, and touched the border of his garment: and immediately her issue of blood stanched. And Jesus said, Who touched me? When all denied, Peter and they that were with him said, Master, the multitude throng thee and press thee, and sayest thou, Who touched me? And Jesus said, Somebody hath touched me: for I perceive that virtue is gone out of me. And when the woman saw that she was not hid, she came trembling, and falling down before him, she declared unto him before all the people for what cause she had touched him, and how she was healed immediately.

This woman had "spent all her living" without success. Her money, her efforts, and her doctors couldn't cure her. There was nothing she could do that would alleviate her problem. The only thing she had left to do was to throw herself on the mercy of God and the grace of Jesus Christ, and hope that the Lord would restore her health. The Lord Jesus, as God manifest in the flesh, was full of grace, and she needed Him to bestow grace upon her. So she came up behind Him in the crowd and touched His garment—but so did many others that were in the crowd. That is why the disciples were bewildered that He noticed one touch among so many. The Bible says that Jesus sensed virtue had gone out of Him with that touch. Why? Because she touched Him in faith, believing that He would heal her. So the Lord said to her, "Daughter, be of good comfort: *thy faith hath made thee whole*; go in peace." This woman is the type of a sinner who is sin sick and who honestly acknowledges her condition. She comes to Jesus and reaches out to Him in faith, and she is saved. How does one find eternal security here? Because when Jesus heals, the disease does not just go into remission—it goes away altogether, and the subject is cured of that disease forever; physical healing and salvation is permanent. And when Jesus saves a soul, the sinner is cured of the disease of sin forever; spiritual healing and salvation is also permanent.

We can say that our faith is the thing that bridges the gap between our need of God's mercy and forgiveness and God's provision for that forgiveness. There is a specific point in time where the lost sinner, through faith in the Lord Jesus Christ, conducts an eternal transaction, whereby his need of forgiveness meets God's atoning provision. The very moment we believe that Christ died for *our* sins and that His work on the Cross is all that we are depending upon for the forgiveness of our sins, we are saved. Faith is simply the way a lost sinner says yes to God's offer of salvation. Faith is the hand that receives the gift of eternal life.

In opposing the teaching of eternal security and demeaning the Bible truth of salvation by grace through faith, the Arminian advocate Purkiser further attempts to bolster his argument by saying, "Eternal life, apparently, is not a cut-and-dried affair sealed at conversion."[22] Again he says, "Nowhere does the Bible suggest that a person who one time believed in Christ is by that past-tense faith assured of final salvation."[23] Yet the very verse he uses to refute this, Ephesians 1:13 (claiming that "once saved, always saved" advocates quote it wrongly), says that very thing. The verse reads as follows: "In whom ye also *trusted*, after that *ye heard* the word of truth, the gospel of your salvation: in whom also *after that ye believed*, ye were *sealed* with that holy Spirit of promise." Notice the past tenses of the verbs used! Those who have been saved "heard the word" (past tense), "trusted" and "believed" (both past tense), and "were sealed" (past tense). All these verbs are past tense and result in the Christian being sealed (past tense) until a future date (Ephesians 4:30—"until the day of redemption").

In his book *Stop Asking Jesus into Your Heart*, J. D. Greear clearly illustrates the principle of one-time believing for salvation this way: "If you are seated right now, there was a point in time in which you transferred the weight of your body from your legs to the chair. ... Salvation is a posture of repentance and faith toward the finished work of Christ, in which you transfer the weight of your hopes of heaven off of your own righteousness and onto the finished work of Jesus Christ. ... The posture begins at a moment [when you trusted Christ], but it persists for a lifetime. ... There is a moment where you transfer your hope of heaven from your own merits to Christ's substitutionary work."[24] This posture of repentance and faith is what saves. We who are saved are resting in Christ and pinning our hope of heaven on Jesus Christ and what He did for us on the Cross and by His resurrection. To quote Mr. Finney again, we secure our salvation from God "by one act of faith, [when we] receive Jesus Christ as He is offered in the Gospel."

## THE MEANING OF SALVATION

The Bible plainly declares the meaning of salvation in Ephesians 1, verse 10. "For we are his workmanship, created in Christ Jesus unto good works, which God hath before ordained that we should walk in them."

In other words, the reader is told what the purpose is for God saving sinners. The *reason* is because of His love, mercy, and grace, but the *purpose* is that Christians might glorify Him with their lives here on earth (as the old saying goes, "Those who are saved by grace ought not to live a life of disgrace") and then throughout eternity.

The Lord saves lost sinners that they might be "to the praise of the glory of his grace, wherein he hath made us accepted in the beloved. In whom we have redemption through his blood, the forgiveness of sins, according to the riches of his grace" (Ephesians 1:6, 7), and "that in the ages to come he might shew [*demonstrate, display, exhibit, 'show off'*] the exceeding riches of his grace in his kindness toward us through Christ Jesus" (Ephesians 2:7).

As God's workmanship, every believer is a product of His making. Every Christian is an "original creation" of the heavenly potter, who has been made by Him, for His glory, and for His use. Those who have been born again are "new creature(s)" in Christ (2 Corinthians 5:17) and have been "created in Christ Jesus unto good works." Notice that God's people are not saved *by* good works (Ephesians 2:9) but are saved *unto* good works. As a matter of fact, Christians have been "before ordained" by God to live their lives characterized by good works that will be seen by the world and therewith glorify their Father which is in heaven (Matthew 5:16). Not only are Christians *predestinated* to be conformed to the image of Christ (Romans 8:29), but also it's equally true that believers are *preordained* to live godly lives for Christ. And when God's children walk in those good works, in obedience to the commands of Christ, they can experience the assurance of salvation. The apostle John wrote in the context of walking with Christ: "And hereby we do know that we know him, if we keep his commandments" (1 John 2:3). Please notice the verse does not say that "we know Him, if we keep His commandments," but it says. "Hereby we do know that know him." He is talking about the believer's *assurance* of salvation and not salvation itself. (That is, salvation and knowing Christ as Savior does not depend on the Christian's obedience, but *assurance* does. If the child of God does not "live right," it's very possible that they may doubt whether they are truly saved or not.)

The statement has been made that eternal security is inherently taught in the doctrine of salvation by grace. How? Well, those saved by grace must of necessity be kept by grace.

One of the great hymns of the faith is titled "Grace Greater Than Our Sin." This song brings to mind the thought of Romans

5:20, where the Bible says that "where sin did abound, grace did much more abound." In other words, if there is a sin that can be committed that would cause one to "lose salvation," then both the song and the Bible verse are wrong. If there is a sin that can cost a redeemed and regenerated child of God his salvation, then that sin is greater than the grace of God; the sin would abound more than the grace of God. But the Bible is right, and the song is correct. There's no sin that can damn a Christian, because the grace of God *is* greater than all my sin, and the greater the sin, whether in number or degree, the greater the grace of God to cover that sin.

Since salvation is by grace, then there is nothing one can do to deserve, earn or merit the favor of God. If one cannot "get saved" by his works, then how could one "lose it" because of his works? Those who are counting on their works to get them to heaven are never sure of salvation while those who *do not* count on their works to save them *can* be certain of salvation and have that assurance in their hearts. It is not the *believer's* faith that saves him, but *Christ's* faith (Galatians 2:16 with Ephesians 2:8's "and *that* not of yourselves," referring to faith). It is not the *Christian's* works that save him, but *Christ's* work on Calvary that saves.

One of my former pastors told this story that illustrates the thoughts of this chapter in a humorous way: Two men walked into a barbershop that was run by a German couple, Verks Verner and his wife, Grace. They both got a shave and a haircut, one by Mr. Verner and the other by Mrs. Verner. A week later, one of the men called the other to see if he was ready to go back for another trim and a shave, but his friend told him, no, he was fine, and didn't need either. So the man went back, and Mr. Verner gave him another trim and shave. Another week went by. He called his friend, thinking surely he would be ready by now. But again, his friend said he still looked clean shaven. So when he went back into the barbershop, he asked Mr. Verner, "What is the deal here? My friend has gone three weeks without having to come back and is still clean shaven, and I have to come in every week." Mr. Verner answered him (in his German accent): "Vell, ven you're shaved by Verks, you have to be shaved and shaved all over again. But ven you are shaved by Grace, it's vonce shaved, alvays shaved."

Christians can say with Simon Peter, "But we believe that through the grace of the Lord Jesus Christ we shall be saved" (Acts 15:11).

# SITUATED IN THE BODY

*So we, being many, are one body in Christ, and every one members one of another.*
—ROMANS 12:5

*And he is the head of the body, the church.*
—COLOSSIANS 1:18

The Christian is a member of a body whose head is the Lord Jesus Christ (Romans 12:5). This body is the Church, and the head is the supreme leader of the Church, Jesus Christ (Colossians 1:18). Christ, as the head of the Church, is "the intelligent director" and "the authoritative lawgiver" of the Church.[25]

The word *body* is used in two distinct ways in reference to the Church of the Lord Jesus Christ.

It is used in a functional sense, being defined as "a group of individuals organized for some purpose,"[26] as in a legislative *body*. The church is an organization of people, a body of believers, with and for a purpose, who assemble themselves together, in order to plan and carry out that purpose. (The purpose of a true

New Testament church is threefold: to evangelize the world, to educate its converts, and to exalt its Savior, Jesus Christ.)

The word *body* is also used in a metaphorical sense. The Bible uses figurative language to describe believers as members of Christ's body, which is the Church. For example, in 1 Corinthians 12, the apostle Paul uses the symbolism of a body as an illustration of the Church and the Christian's relation to it, to one another and to Christ Himself. He speaks of individual Christians as "members" and makes mention of an "eye" and an "ear" and of a "foot" and a "hand." In this section, the doctrine of eternal security will be studied in light of the metaphorical usage.

The born-again child of God should be a member of that spiritual organization known as the local, visible New Testament church. Whether he is or not, each Christian *is* a part of the spiritual organism known as the universal body of Christ (what the writer of Hebrews calls "the general assembly and church of the firstborn" [12:23]) by virtue of a spiritual union with its head, Jesus Christ. It isn't just an association but a vital relationship, where the sinner and the Savior are two separate individuals who come together and become one. This thought is expressed in the biblical analogy of marriage, where Christ is the bridegroom and the Church is the bride, and they are one day to be married (see Ephesians 5 and Revelation 19, 21). The scripture states in 1 Corinthians 6:15–17 that the Christians' "bodies are the members of Christ" and then compares the believer's relationship to Christ with that of a physical union, saying, "For two, saith he, shall be one flesh." It is understood that an earthly, physical union is when two become one in the flesh and that such a one-time act constitutes a "joining," or in other words, a marriage. On a higher level, the same passage says in verse 17, "But he that is joined unto the Lord is one spirit." Thus, the Bible teaches that the Christian and Jesus Christ are joined together in a spiritual union, and one we would say that is an eternal union.

In the following paragraphs, three aspects of the biblical concept of the believer in Christ and the body of Christ as it relates to the doctrine of eternal security will be discussed.

## THE CHRISTIAN IS SITUATED IN CHRIST

The phrase "in Christ" occurs numerous times in the New Testament and is familiar to any Bible reader. The Christian is in a *vital union* with Christ. He is literally "in Christ." The apostle Paul wrote to the church at Ephesus, "Blessed be the God and Father of our Lord Jesus Christ, who hath blessed us with all spiritual blessings in heavenly places *in Christ*" (Ephesians 1:3). Again, to the Corinthian church, he wrote, "Therefore if any man be *in Christ*, he is a new creature: old things are passed away; behold, all things are become new" (2 Corinthians 5:17).

In God's ledger of humanity, every man, woman, boy, and girl falls under one of two headings. A person is either "in Adam" or "in Christ." Those in Adam are lost, without hope and without God, because they are without Christ. Those who are in Christ are saved because they have received the Lord Jesus as their personal Savior. The Bible says in 1 Corinthians 15:22, "For as *in Adam* all die, even so *in Christ* shall all be made alive."

Every human being is initially conceived "in sin" (Psalm 51:5), born spiritually dead *in sin* (Ephesians 2:1), and considered to be what the Bible refers to as "in Adam." Adam, the first man and the first sinner, is referred to as the federal head of the unregenerate human race. From him, all of his descendants have inherited sinful natures, along with both physical and spiritual death sentences. The apostle Paul noted in Romans 5:12, "Wherefore, as *by one man sin entered into the world*, and *death by sin*; and so *death passed upon all men*, for that *all have sinned.*" Again, in Romans 3:23, the Bible says, "All have sinned." The result of man's sins is "death" (Romans 6:23): physical death that consigns the body to the earth from whence it came, and spiritual death that condemns the soul to hell from where there is no escape. "In Adam," the sinner stands condemned before a holy God, without any righteousness to call his own.

At this point, the reader is directed to a very important truth: every human being's history is founded upon and springs from Adam's personal history. The same is true of the believer's relationship to Christ. Because of the believer's union with Christ, every born-again Christian is "in Him;" and, therefore, His history is theirs. Just as unbelievers are *condemned sinners* "in Adam," so believers are *justified saints* "in Christ."

Notice the contrast and explanation that Paul gives in Romans 5. The *contrast* is between the causes and effects of the actions of the first Adam and the last Adam, Jesus Christ. The *explanation* is that Jesus Christ *undid* and *remedied* what Adam did in the Garden of Eden. In verses 18 and 19 of that chapter, the Bible says, "Therefore as by the offence of one [Adam] judgment came upon all men to condemnation; even so by the righteousness of one [Christ] the free gift came upon all men unto justification of life. For as by one man's disobedience [Adam's] many were made sinners, so by the obedience of one [Christ] shall many be made righteous."

Further, observe how the believer's position in Christ is personalized. In Galatians 2:20, the word of God says that every

Christian is *"crucified with Christ,"* yet is alive and living "in the flesh." The great Chinese Christian, Watchman Nee, wrote, "The Lord Jesus was crucified outside Jerusalem nearly two thousand years ago, and I *was crucified with Him.* This is the great historic fact. By it his experience has now become my spiritual history."[27] Also, in Romans 6:3, the Bible says that every Christian has been "baptized *into Jesus Christ"* and "into his death." Again, Mr. Nee states, "Our union with Christ began ... with his death. God included us in him there. We were 'with him' because we were 'in him.'"[28]

The moment lost sinners receive Christ and are saved, the Spirit of God baptizes them into the body of Christ, His Church. The Bible teaches in 1 Corinthians 12:13 that "by one Spirit are we all baptized into one body, whether we be Jews or Gentiles, whether we be bond or free; and have been all made to drink into one Spirit." The believer in Christ has been baptized (placed) by the Holy Ghost into the body of Christ, the Church. Mr. Nee states, "God has put us in Christ. What happened to him happened also to us. All the experiences he met, we too have met *in him."*[29] The born-again believer's history "was written in Christ before we were born. ... Our deliverance from sin is based, not on what we can do, nor even on what God is going to do for us, but on what he has already done for us in Christ."[30]

The apostle John said in 1 John 4:17, "Herein is our love made perfect, that we may have boldness in the Day of Judgment: because *as he is, so are we in this world."* As Jesus is at this moment, so are the saved in this world because they are "in Him." According to the Bible, the Lord Jesus Christ was crucified, and so too is the Christian; He was buried, and so too is the Christian; He is risen, and so too is the Christian; He is seated at the right hand of God the Father, and so too is the Christian; He is righteous, sinless and holy, and so too is the Christian. All these things apply to the individual Christian by virtue of his position "in Christ," and it is all "of God," not of ourselves. As the Bible says in 1 Corinthians 1:30, "But *of him* are ye *in Christ Jesus*, who *of God* is *made unto us* wisdom, and righteousness, and sanctification, and redemption."

Again, because of the believer's position "in Christ," Christians have certain blessings those outside the fold of salvation do not possess. Jesus Christ is the believer's wisdom, righteousness, sanctification, and redemption. This is what the Psalmist meant when he said: "The LORD is ... *my salvation*" (Psalm 27:1). Jesus is all a sinner needs to get to heaven.

Please notice what the Bible says in Romans 8:29–30: "For whom he did foreknow, he also did predestinate to be conformed to the image of his Son, that he might be the firstborn among many brethren. Moreover whom he did *predestinate*, them he also *called*: and whom he called, them he also *justified*: and whom he justified, them he also *glorified*."

Notice the progression of the acts of God in relation to the believer "in Christ." The order begins with foreknowledge, followed by predestination, then by the calling, the justification, and finally the glorification of the saint. The careful reader will observe that each of these actions is referred to in the past tense, as if each act was performed upon the believer in the past, including the glorification of the saint. If that is true, and it is, then in God's mind the Christian is *already* glorified, which cannot be possible unless it is something that God reckons to be true already. One Christian author explains the truth of eternal security found in Romans 8:30 this way: "The Bible indicates that once a person becomes a part of the family of God by trusting in Christ, he is absolutely secure. ... Here [*Romans 8:30*] there is an unbroken chain of events from predestination to glorification in heaven, and *past tenses are used to emphasize the certainty of our final glorification.*"[31] Dr. Harold Tabb, commenting on Christians being glorified doctrinally in Christ, says, "Even though we have not yet arrived in heaven to be glorified with Jesus Christ (Romans 8:17), the certainty of our arrival there is shown in the fact that as far as God is concerned, He has *already* glorified us."[32]

Born-again Christians have been translated out of one kingdom and into another. Paul wrote in his epistle to the Colossians (1:13) that God has "delivered us from the power of darkness, and hath translated us into the kingdom of his dear Son." In the Old Testament, in Genesis chapter five, the Bible says that Enoch was literally translated (i.e., changed from one state to another and from one station, location, or position to another). Christians have been translated in the sense that their station and position has been changed. The Christian has been translated from his position "in Adam" to a new state of being "in Christ." The believer's position of being situated "in Christ" is another Bible assurance of the Christian's eternal security.

## THE CHRISTIAN IS SEATED WITH CHRIST

After His crucifixion and resurrection, the Lord Jesus spent forty days with His disciples, instructing them in the things concerning the kingdom of God (Acts 1:3). Then He ascended to heaven (Acts 1:9) and sat down on the right hand of God the Father. The Bible says in Mark 16:19, "So then after the Lord had spoken unto them, he was received up into heaven, and *sat on the right hand of God."* In 1 Peter 3:22, the scriptures state that the Lord Jesus Christ "is gone into heaven, and is *on the right hand of God*; angels and authorities and powers being made subject unto him." In Hebrews 1:3, the Bible says of the Lord Jesus Christ, "Who being the brightness of his [God's] glory, and the express image of his [God's] person, and upholding all things by the word of his power, when he had by himself purged our sins, *sat down on the right hand of the Majesty on high."* In the Epistle to the Ephesians (1:20–21) Paul wrote that "[God] raised [Jesus] from the dead, and *set him at his own right hand in the heavenly places*, Far above all principality, and power, and might, and dominion, and every name that is named, not only in this world, but also in that which is to come."

The child of God enjoys a unique position. It has been learned from the discussion in the previous section that Christians are situated "in Christ." But not only that, believers are also *"seated with Christ,"* in heaven itself, already!

In the same letter to the Ephesians (2:4–6) the word of God says, "But God, who is rich in mercy, for his great love wherewith he loved us, Even when we were dead in sins, hath *quickened us together with Christ*, (by grace ye are saved;) And hath *raised us up together*, and made us *sit together* in heavenly places *in Christ Jesus."* Watchman Nee wrote, "God has first by His mighty power 'made Him (Christ) to sit,' and then by grace 'made us sit with Him.'"[33]

There is an interesting statement found in Jesus's conversation with Nicodemus in John chapter 3. In the last half of verse 13, Jesus clearly says that He was in two places at once. (Here, it is obvious that the Lord Jesus claimed one of the attributes of deity—omnipresence. Unfortunately, this statement is not found in the modern "Bible" versions.) The scriptural truth is that, just as Jesus our Lord and Savior was *on earth* and *in heaven* at the *same time*, even so are believers now! A believer in Christ is a believer actually in Christ by virtue of his or her faith in the Savior, and through the baptism of the Holy Ghost at the moment of salvation (1 Corinthians 12:13). The believer's *geographical location* is here on this earth, in a body of flesh, but his *spiritual position* is "in heavenly places in Christ Jesus." While a Christian may be seated in the pew at church, or on the couch at the house, or in the chair behind a desk at work, he is in a spiritual yet literal sense also seated at the right hand of God the Father "in Christ Jesus."

While Christians are at home in the body, and absent from the Lord, yet they are on the earth and in heavenly places simultaneously. They are both *literally* "in the flesh" physically, and in Christ *spiritually*, at the same time. Those who are saved are "in Christ," seated at the right hand of God the Father, in "heavenly places," right now at this very moment, for all eternity! This being true, the Christian, really, is just as good as in heaven *as if he were already there* "with the door shut and the key thrown away." The Christian is eternally secure because he is in Christ and seated with Him beside the Father in Heaven right now.

[As an added thought, since the Christian is in the body of Christ, which currently is upon the earth, and Christ is the head of the Church, and He is in Heaven, the members of His body, Christians, are safe. This is true because as long as your head is above water, you won't drown.]

## THE CHRISTIAN CANNOT BE SEVERED FROM CHRIST

The Bible says in Ephesians 5:30, "For we are members of his body, of his flesh, and of his bones." The Christian's position in

Christ places him in such a condition that for the child of God to "lose salvation" is a completely *impossible situation*.

On the road to Damascus, en route to torment the Christian population there, Saul (later called Paul) was confronted by Jesus Christ. The Lord asked Saul, the oppressor of the Church, "Saul, Saul, why persecutest thou me?" (Acts 9:4) and went on to say to him, "I am Jesus whom thou persecutest" (Acts 9:5). What this means is that to persecute the Church of Jesus Christ is to persecute Jesus Christ Himself. Just as the LORD Jehovah said that those who harm Israel "toucheth … the apple of his eye" (Zechariah 2:8), even so those who harm the Church are assaulting the Lord Jesus Christ Himself personally. This is because Jesus considers the Church His body, and by extension, one could say that individual Christians are parts of His body. The apostle Paul uses this analogy in 1 Corinthians 12 where he describes the "one body" as having "many [*individual*] members."

The Baptist Hiscox comments on the Christian's relation to the body of Christ: "The figure [*of the body of Christ*] indicates the intimate, sensitive, and sacred relation existing between Christ and his people."[34] The Bible teaches in 1 Corinthians 12:13 that believers are placed into the body of Christ by the Spirit of God the moment they place their trust in Christ and are saved. Christians literally become a part of the spiritual, mystical, universal, and invisible "body of Christ," which is the Church (Ephesians 1:21–22). This being the case, if the individual Christian is a part of Christ's body, for the child of God to "lose salvation" would be the equivalent of a person being offended by a part of his body and lopping it off to remove the offending member. For the Christian to "lose salvation," he would have to be removed from his position in Christ's body; as morbidly vulgar as it sounds, Jesus Christ would have to cut off a part of His body to remove the offending member. It would be a sort of divine, spiritual amputation.

Consider what the Bible says in 2 Timothy 2:11–13. "It is a faithful saying: For if we be dead with him, we shall also live with him: If we suffer, we shall also reign with him: if we deny him, he also will deny us: If we believe not, yet he abideth faithful: *he cannot deny himself.*" The Lord will not deny Himself, and since the Christian is in Christ and actually a part of His body, even if a believer were to *stop* believing in Him and *deny* Him (as Simon Peter did!), He cannot and will not "deny Himself." Genuine Christians are safe "in Him." For Him to deny a believer in Him would be to deny His own "flesh and bones." How totally absurd it is to think or teach that Jesus our Savior would sever one of the members of His body.

## THE CHRISTIAN IS SAFE IN THE HANDS OF GOD

From a doctrinal point of view, after Calvary, every believer is *a part* of His hand (Ephesians 5:30), but from a devotional aspect, the children of God are pictured as being *in His hands.*

The apostle John recorded these famous words of Jesus in chapter 10, verses 27 to 30 of his Gospel: "My sheep hear my voice, and I know them, and they follow me: And I give unto them eternal life; and they shall never perish, neither shall any man pluck them out of my hand. My Father, which gave them me, is greater than all; and no man is able to pluck them out of my Father's hand. I and my Father are one."

According to what Christ taught in this passage of scripture, He gives eternal life to His sheep. The Lord Jesus Christ is the

"Shepherd and Bishop of our souls" and His "sheep" refers to God's people, the saved, those who have turned to the Lord for salvation. (1 Peter 2:25; Psalm 100:3)

Jesus says that He gives eternal life to His sheep. Notice that this life is *eternal* life. Eternal life is *eternal*, and therefore one who has life that is eternal will live eternally. This eternal life is a "gift" that is given to those who hear and heed His voice. When the lost sheep returns to Christ the shepherd, he receives the *gift* of eternal life (Romans 6:23b). Since "the gifts and calling of God are without repentance" (Romans 11:29), the members of His flock can be sure that God will not "take back" the salvation He has given them. The God of the Bible is not an "Indian giver."

The Bible teaches that God the Father and God the Son both hold each individual Christian in their hands. Jesus spoke of "my hand" (verse 28) and "my Father's hand" (verse 29). The picture is that of the Christian being held in Christ's hand and the Father's hand. It is as if God the Father and Jesus the Son have joined hands and the Christian is clasped between their hands and "in the grip of God." How secure is that? The believer in Christ, once saved, and in God's grip of grace, cannot be "plucked out" of their hands: no one can take a Christian out of their firm grip—no church, denomination, not even the devil, can pry any of God's children out of Their hands.

An insurance company has an old and familiar sales slogan that sounds reassuring to its clients. It could be modified to say: "You're in good hands *with the Almighty!*"

Because of the believer's situation in Christ, he can be certain of being eternally secure "in Him."

# SEALED BY THE HOLY SPIRIT

*In whom ye also trusted, after that ye heard the word of truth, the gospel of your salvation: in whom also after that ye believed, ye were sealed with that holy Spirit of promise, Which is the earnest of our inheritance until the redemption of the purchased possession, unto the praise of his glory.*

—EPHESIANS 1:13, 14

In respect to the doctrine of eternal security, the word *seal* is noteworthy. In the Bible a seal signifies (1) a finished transaction, (2) ownership, and (3) security.[35]

## SIGNIFIES SECURITY

Scripture with scripture (for the Bible is its own best commentator), notice that the same writer, the apostle Paul, in the same epistle, clearly verifies the duration of this sealing of the Holy Spirit.

Observe chapter 4, verse 30: "And grieve not the holy Spirit of God, whereby ye are sealed *unto the day of redemption.*" The born-again believer is sealed by the Spirit of God *until the day of redemption.*

Now, many God-loving, church-going, faithful Christians would not understand this verse, and would identify the day of redemption as either the death of Christ at Calvary or the day they received Christ as Savior and were redeemed. Of course, this would be very confusing to the average Bible-illiterate church member. This misunderstanding implies that either the seal received at the moment of salvation was only up until Calvary or the seal was only until the day of the individual's conversion. Either idea can be dismissed as being illogical and nonsensical. This sealing cannot mean until Calvary, which is looking to the past, and it cannot mean only up to the moment that one is regenerated because no one is sealed by the Holy Spirit before they are actually saved. The interpretation must be that the sealing takes place at conversion and is in place until a future "day of redemption." The day that Christ died He purchased man's salvation through redemption and the day that any lost sinner was saved ("the day of salvation"—2 Corinthians 6:2), his spirit was regenerated and his soul was redeemed, but neither one of those days is the "day of redemption" Paul is talking about in these verses. The "day of redemption" he is speaking of will occur at the rapture of the church.

In Romans 13:11–12, it is said that "our salvation [is] nearer than when we believed," and that "the day is at hand," or near. So, in some respect, even though a believer was saved on a particular day sometime in the past, whether it was twenty years ago, two years ago, two weeks ago, or two days ago, each believer is, with each passing moment, that much closer to the day of his ultimately completed salvation. This is another reference indicating that, like redemption, salvation is not completely obtained at the moment of conversion. There is a future day when the Christian will "obtain {salvation and glory} by our Lord Jesus Christ" (1 Timothy 5:9; 2 Thessalonians 2:14). There is day coming when "the trial of your faith, being much more precious than of gold that perisheth, though it be tried with fire, might be found unto praise and honour and glory *at the appearing of Jesus Christ*: Whom having not seen, ye love; in whom, though now ye see him not, yet believing, ye rejoice with joy unspeakable and full of glory: *Receiving the end of your faith, even the salvation of your souls*" (1 Peter 1:7–9). In 1 Thessalonians 5:23, the apostle's prayer is that God would "sanctify you *wholly*" and that the Christian's "*whole* spirit and soul and body [would] be preserved blameless unto the coming of our Lord Jesus Christ." From these verses, it's evident that salvation, although it was accomplished at Calvary and is personally received when one "gets saved," yet there is a future culmination that is called the "day of redemption," when believers will be completely, finally, and forever redeemed and saved—the individual's entire body, soul, and spirit; the "whole kit and caboodle," one could say. And that day will be when the Lord Jesus Christ returns for His church at the rapture, which precedes the great tribulation and His second advent proper at Armageddon. That will be when the "redemption of the purchased possession" (Ephesians 1:14) takes place. In the book of Romans, chapter 8, verses 18–23, the Bible further elaborates this truth:

> For I reckon that the sufferings of this present time are not worthy to be compared with *the*

*glory which shall be revealed in us.* For the earnest expectation of the creature *waiteth for the manifestation of the sons of God.* For the creature was made subject to vanity, not willingly, but by reason of him who hath subjected the same in hope, Because the creature itself also shall be delivered from the bondage of corruption into *the glorious liberty of the children of God.* For we know that the whole creation groaneth and travaileth in pain together until now. And not only they, but ourselves also, which have the firstfruits of the Spirit, even we ourselves groan within ourselves, *waiting for the adoption, to wit, the redemption of our body.*

When a person receives Jesus Christ as his or her personal Savior, the person's spirit is "saved" and his soul is "saved," but the *body* is still unsaved and unredeemed. When Christ returns, the Christian's salvation will be completed, when the believer receives the end of his faith and obtains the salvation of Jesus Christ with glory.

The Bible teaches that God's people can be "confident of this very thing, that he which hath begun a good work in [them] will perform it until the day of Jesus Christ" (Philippians 1:6). Believers are sealed by the Holy Spirit until that "good work" is completed, and then the seal will be removed, and all God's children will be "conformed to the image of Christ" (Romans 8:29, 30).

According to the Lord's half-brother, Christians "are sanctified by God the Father, and *preserved* in Jesus Christ" (Jude

1). He goes on to say in verse 24 that the Lord is able to "present [us] faultless before the presence of his glory with exceeding joy."

Dr. Scofield connects the above verses dealing with the Christian's preservation in Christ and presentation by Christ with the believer's assurance of eternal salvation, and says: "Assurance is the believer's full conviction that, through the work of Christ alone, received by faith, *he is in possession of a salvation in which he will be eternally kept.*"[36]

Dr. Stanley suggests that if salvation in Christ is not permanent, as illustrated by the symbol of the seal, then the Lord would be treating His bride (see Ephesians 5) like a man who gives "a woman an engagement ring when he knows he has no intention of marrying her."[37] Surely, the God of the Bible would not give believers the pledge of eternal life if He were not sure that they would remain eternally His.

(The reader might also read John 14:16 in this connection, where the Lord told the disciples that when the Comforter, which is the Holy Ghost, comes to the believer, He does so that "he may abide with you *for ever.*" The New Testament believer in Christ has eternal security because the Spirit of God that indwells him will abide with him "for ever." The Christian in this current church-age dispensation has a promise of the perpetual abiding of the Holy Spirit that even King David, who had the "sure mercies" [Isaiah 55:3; Acts 13:34], did not know of [Psalm 51:11] as it was not revealed until the New Testament.)

To summarize this section, the Lord "seals" every believer at conversion and until Christ returns and transforms him into His very image. In other words, Christians are *preserved* until the Rapture, and then will be *perfected* forever, when God the Father conforms all believers into the image of His own Son, and they are made to be like Jesus Christ.

Using the Bible as its own best dictionary, the Scriptures also indicate that when something is sealed, it is thereafter unchanging and unchangeable. Notice how the term "sealed" is used in Daniel 6:17: "And a stone was brought, and laid upon the mouth of the den; and *the king sealed it with his own signet*, and with the signet of his lords; *that the purpose might not be changed* concerning Daniel." Once a thing is sealed by the King, the purpose cannot be changed.[38] Once God seals the believer in Christ by His Spirit, the believer's salvation is sure and secure because the king's seal renders it an *unalterable* and *irreversible* act.

## SIGNIFIES A FINISHED TRANSACTION AND OWNERSHIP

The text says that the "holy Spirit of promise" (verse 13) is the *"earnest of our inheritance* until the redemption of the purchased possession" (verse 14). In the book of 2 Corinthians, chapter 5, the same writer says that the Lord has given believers the *"earnest of the Spirit"* (verse 5), and it is in the context of the new body to be received at the rapture of the Church. The Second Epistle to the Corinthians, in chapter one and verse 22, says that God "hath also sealed us, and given us the *earnest of the Spirit* in our hearts."

An "earnest" is defined as "something given as security or guaranty for the performance of an act" or "something of value given by a buyer to a seller to bind a bargain."[39] It is like the deposit a buyer puts down to hold an item before it is fully paid for and claimed, or as Paul says, "until the redemption of the purchased possession" (Ephesians 1:14).[40]

There is a perfect illustration of this found in the book of Jeremiah (chapter 32:6–14):

And Jeremiah said, The word of the LORD came unto me, saying, Behold, Hanameel the son of Shallum thine uncle shall come unto thee saying, Buy thee my field that is in Anathoth: for the right of redemption is thine to buy it. So Hanameel mine uncle's son came to me in the court of the prison according to the word of the LORD, and said unto me, Buy my field, I pray thee, that is in Anathoth, which is in the country of Benjamin: for the right of inheritance is thine, and the redemption is thine; buy it for thyself. Then I knew that this was the word of the LORD. And I bought the field of Hanameel my uncle's son, that was in Anathoth, and weighed him the money, even seventeen shekels of silver. *And I subscribed the evidence, and sealed it, and took witnesses, and weighed him the money in the balances.* So I took the *evidence of the purchase,* both that which was *sealed* according to the law and custom, and that which was open: And I gave the *evidence of the purchase* unto Baruch the son of Neriah, the son of Maaseiah, in the sight of Hanameel mine uncle's son, and in the presence of the witnesses that *subscribed the book of the purchase,* before all the Jews that sat in the court of the prison. And I charged Baruch before them, saying, Thus saith the LORD of hosts, the God of

Israel; Take these evidences, this *evidence of the purchase*, both which is *sealed*, and this evidence which is open; and put them in an earthen vessel, that they may continue many days.

In the passage, there is merchandise (a "field," property, real estate), a seller, a buyer, and witnesses. The buyer purchases the property; the procedure is to subscribe the evidence, seal it, and pay the money, all in the sight of witnesses.

The word *subscribe* means "to sign a document" as a pledge to fulfill a financial obligation, with the amount annotated in the document. In the case of Jeremiah, the "evidence of purchase" was like a "bill of sale." He bought and paid for the property for a certain amount of money. As evidence of his purchase, he signed a legal document in the presence of witnesses, and then it was "sealed," or notarized as it is known today. The sealing of the document attested to the fact that the transaction was legitimate, legal, and in order. So in this instance the seal signifies a *finished transaction*.

This means that when God saves and seals a repentant, believing sinner by His Spirit that He puts down the "earnest money" for the "purchased possession" (the Christian is the purchased possession). The "earnest" is the "down payment," the deposit, so to speak. The "seal" indicates that the Christian *has been* "purchased" and *now* belongs to the Lord. As stated in 2 Timothy 2:19a, "Nevertheless the foundation of God standeth sure, *having this **seal**, The Lord knoweth them that are his.*" Every Christian has God's stamp on his soul, claiming them for His own. God is not going to discard or throw away His purchased possession that He has bought and paid for, signed for and sealed with His own signet. Believers are His and belong to Him (Romans 8:9). Salvation is a "done deal" for all the redeemed.

On the Cross, just before He died, the Lord Jesus cried out, "It is finished" (John 19:30). Jesus was testifying to the fact that the work of redemption was done. His mission was accomplished, so that we can assuredly say that the debt of sin has been paid in full, and it is an eternally completed, finished transaction. To cite a familiar preacher's cliché: "We owed a debt we could not pay, He paid a debt He did not owe."

The old-time Methodist preacher, Rev. Frank M. Graham, wrote one of the Church's favorite revival hymns. His gospel song describes the truth of saving faith in Christ. It goes like this:

> There was a time on earth, when in the book of heaven,
> An old account was standing, for sins yet unforgiven;
> The old account was large and growing every day,
> I went unto the keeper and settled long ago.
> Long ago, long ago – Yes, the old account was settled long ago.
> And the record's clear today, for He washed my sins away,
> When the old account was settled long ago.

The phrase "It is finished" is the translation of one Greek word, *tetelestai*. In the Greek language, this phrase is the victor's cry of triumph. It is also a merchant's term that signified a finished transaction, a completed purchase.[41] When a buyer purchased an item with cash, or made a final payment, the seller would write on the sales receipt, at the top of the bill of sale, "Tetelestai," which meant "Paid in full." When Jesus died on the Cross and shed His precious blood, the world's eternal salvation was purchased, bought and paid for. Redeemed sinners owe nothing because *Jesus paid it all!*

The consequence and result of Christ's death on the Cross is eternal salvation. The Bible says in Hebrews 10:10, 12, 14, 17, and 18:

> By the which will we are sanctified through the offering of the body of Jesus Christ *once for all*. But this man, after he had offered one sacrifice for sins *for ever*, sat down on the right hand of God; For by one offering he hath *perfected for ever* them that are sanctified. And their sins and iniquities will I remember no more. Now where remission of these is, there is *no more* offering for sin.

The truth of eternal security is inherent in the historical act and doctrinal fact of Christ's substitutionary death, burial, and resurrection for lost sinners. In that Jesus died to pay the penalty of sin for the world's transgressions, the Bible says that believers are "sanctified through the offering of the body of Jesus Christ *once for all*" (Hebrews 10:10) – because "it is finished." "After he had offered one sacrifice for sins *for ever*, [He] sat down on the right hand of God" (Hebrews 10:12) because the work was done, and – "it is finished." If the reader is a Christian, then he has been "perfected for ever" (Hebrews 10:14) because "it is finished." Once a person's sins have been forgiven, "there is *no more* offering for sin" (Hebrews 10:18) because Jesus said, "It is finished." In plainer words, the sin debt has been paid in full, once and for all, finally and forever.

The seal of God speaks of security, ownership, and preservation. Ron Rhodes, president of Reasoning from the Scriptures Ministries, writes, "In ancient times, a Roman emperor would seal his letter with wax and then stamp it with his own personal seal. That seal would guarantee that the letter would make it to its final destination. Anyone who opened the letter before it arrived at its destination would be put to death. The believer in Jesus is like a letter destined for heaven, and the Holy Spirit (God Himself) is our 'seal,' guaranteeing that we will make it to our final destination."[42]

The sealing of the Holy Spirit guarantees the believer's entrance into heaven.

# THE SURGERY OF THE LORD

*And ye are complete in him, which is the head of all principality and power: In whom also ye are circumcised with the circumcision made without hands, in putting off the body of the sins of the flesh by the circumcision of Christ: Buried with him in baptism, wherein also ye are risen with him through the faith of the operation of God, who hath raised him from the dead. And you, being dead in your sins and the uncircumcision of your flesh, hath he quickened together with him, having forgiven you all trespasses; Blotting out the handwriting of ordinances that was against us, which was contrary to us, and took it out of the way, nailing it to his cross; And having spoiled principalities and powers, he made a shew of them openly, triumphing over them in it.*

—COLOSSIANS 2:10–15

The above passage of scripture contains one of the most interesting doctrinal teachings found in the Bible, yet most Christians know little or nothing about it. Even some who have heard of it, yet have not given it serious consideration, have rejected it out of hand and ridiculed those who teach it. As an example, one detractor cites the following statement by one author: "When the believer is born again, his soul is literally cut loose from the inside of his fleshly body," and remarks that this particular commentator takes spiritual circumcision very literally, then dismisses the idea without any counter argument. He states that he doesn't have to refute this teaching, in that it is "self-refuting for the simple fact that [it has] no biblical authority," and then asks, "Why should we have to refute nonsense?"[43]

Many of that author's Bible teaching contemporaries would agree. I believe the reason for this is that so many ministers literally don't have the time or don't take the time to study their Bibles and are operating solely on what little foundational knowledge they acquired in their three or four years of Bible college, and they're slow to accept anything outside their theological "boxes." This section is going to venture outside that box to see what the Bible actually teaches about this fascinating aspect of eternal security.

To begin, please notice verses 11 and 12:

> In whom also ye are circumcised with the circumcision made without hands, in putting off the body of the sins of the flesh by *the circumcision of Christ*: Buried with him in baptism, wherein also ye are risen with him through the faith of *the operation of God*, who hath raised him from the dead.

In these two verses, the apostle Paul mentions the "operation of God" (verse 12) and the "circumcision of Christ" (11). This operation is not a physical operation. It is spiritual surgery. This is obvious because verse 11 says it is "made *without hands*" (11). [Also, in his discussion about the circumcision that saves apart from the law in Romans chapter 2, Paul says, "*Circumcision is that of the heart, in the spirit*" (verse 29).] The modern-day equivalent could be either laser surgery or laparoscopic assisted surgery. In laparoscopic surgery, the surgeon performs a minimally noninvasive procedure with the aid of advanced medical technology. The doctor's hands don't even touch the patient during the operation, but he inserts the instruments through small incisions into the body and then guides them remotely to look, cut, snip, clamp, and so on.

In a similar fashion, the divine surgeon, Jesus Christ, performs an operation "without hands" on the believing sinner. The general procedure is referred to as an "operation" and the specific procedure is called a "circumcision." Christ is the one who performs the operation and the circumcision because they are said to be "of God" and "of Christ," who is God, and Jesus is the God-man.

To prove the point, context, with a little common sense, will dictate the interpretation of any passage of scripture, including the text under immediate discussion. It also helps to apply the proper rules of grammar. When speaking of the "operation *of* God" and the "circumcision *of* Christ," both God and Christ must be either the *object* of the preposition or the *subject* of the preposition. In both instances, they are no doubt the *subject* of the preposition, the Ones performing the action, not the ones being acted upon (which would be the case if they are the *object* of the preposition). The "operation of God" is not an operation performed *on* God, but an operation performed *by* God upon someone else; and the "circumcision of Christ" is not referring to the procedure that was performed *on* Christ but a procedure that is performed *by* Christ upon someone else. The "someone else" is the patient, who is the Christian, and it takes place at the moment of his new birth. As all surgeons, the Lord Jesus Christ utilizes the surgeon's knife, a scalpel. This of course is the word of God, which is called the "sword of the Spirit" (Ephesians 6:17) and said to be "sharper than any two-edged sword." (Hebrews 4:12)

So far, it should be apparent that there is a spiritual operation (circumcision) that is performed on a sinful patient (a believing sinner) by the Divine Surgeon (Jesus, the God-man) using a supernatural scalpel (the word of God). Now, observe the specific procedure itself.

Verse 11 of Colossians 2 is the primary source for what this specific procedure is. It says, "In whom also ye are circumcised with the circumcision made without hands, in putting off the body of the sins of the flesh by the circumcision of Christ:"

Before salvation, all sinners were "dead in [our] sins and the uncircumcision of [our] flesh" (verse 13), but the moment the Lord Jesus Christ is trusted as Savior and the sinner is saved, believers are "*risen* with him" (12) and "*quickened* [made alive] together with him" (13). As the hymn says, God's love found a way and raised our lives up from out of the dead.[44] This brings to mind what Jesus said to the Jews when they sought to kill Him for healing the impotent man at the pool of Bethesda on the Sabbath day: "Verily, verily, I say unto you, He that heareth my word, and believeth on him that sent me, hath everlasting life, and shall not come into condemnation; but is passed from *death* unto *life.*" (John 5:24)

At the moment of salvation, those who were born "dead in trespasses and sins" (Ephesians 2:1) were "born again" by the Spirit of God (John 3:3–7; John 1:12–13) and given new life in Christ, by Christ, and from Christ (John 5:26; John 10:28). The unbelieving sinner has a live body and a live soul, but a dead spirit. The believing sinner has a live body that God considers dead, "because of sin" and due to his position in Christ (Romans 8:10); a live soul that has been saved from sin; and a spirit that once was dead but that is now alive, because it has been born again and infused with spiritual life.

To properly understand the surgical procedure that God performs, the reader must recognize the difference between the physical and the spiritual. The "operation of God" (verse 11) under consideration is spiritual, and in the context so also are the *burial by baptism* and the fact that born-again believers are *"risen with Him"* (verse 12). At the moment of salvation, when a believing sinner places his faith and trust in Christ as personal Savior, a number of things happen. According to the passage under consideration, Colossians 2:11–12, God performs a spiritual surgery whereby He circumcises the believer and, along with that, buries the new convert with Christ in baptism, raises him up with Christ, quickens him, and forgives him all trespasses. So believers are (1) circumcised, (2) baptized, (3) resurrected [raised], (4) quickened, and (5) forgiven, at the very moment of conversion.

Now, just what happens to the believing sinner during this operation? Again, the proof text, Colossians 2:11, says, "Ye are circumcised with the circumcision made without hands, in putting off the body of the sins of the flesh by the circumcision of Christ." The key to the interpretation is the reference to "circumcision." Those familiar with the Bible know that circumcision was the sign, or token, of the covenant that Jehovah God made with the patriarch Abraham and the nation of Israel (Genesis 17; Romans 2, 4). The word means to "cut" (*cision*) "around" (*circum*). Circumcision, of course, is a common medical procedure to remove the foreskin from the male reproductive member by "cutting around it." This procedure is applied in a figurative sense where God says that mankind needs to be "circumcised in *heart*." It is evident that the real circumcision that is needed is a spiritual one of the heart, and that both men and women can have it (see Romans 2:28, 29).

Now back to the proof text: the circumcision that Christ performs on the believing sinner "[puts] off the body of the sins of the flesh." This seems to indicate that the Lord takes the scalpel of the word of God and "cuts around" the soul, thus removing the body of the sins of the flesh, or more specifically separating the soul from the body of the sins of the flesh. Since sin resides in the flesh (Romans 7:17, 18), once the circumcision is accomplished, the soul and body are "divided asunder" (Hebrews 4:12), separating the body of sin from the soul. This being the case, God has positioned the Christian in such a way that his soul no longer sins—only his "body of the sins of the flesh" does. Therefore, the Christian is exempted from the law of God that states, "The *soul* that sinneth, it shall die" (Ezekiel 18:4, 20). The born-again Christian is not subject to the law of sin and death (Romans 8:2) any longer. The law has no claim on him and cannot condemn him. Again, the reason is that his soul has been circumcised and separated from his flesh, so that his *flesh* sins and suffers physical death, but his *soul* does not sin because it has been sanctified and set apart from the flesh and from sin, and set apart unto God and holiness. The Christian's soul will never die because it will never sin again, and thus the law cannot touch him. He is guiltless, blameless, and even sinless, in the sight of God by virtue of his position in Christ and his relationship to the law.

## WHAT ABOUT 1 JOHN 3:9?

This then explains 1 John 3:9 and clears up the misunderstanding about sinless perfection in this life that some groups teach and refer to as the eradication of the sinful nature. The verse reads: "Whosoever is born of God doth not commit sin; for his seed remaineth in him: and he cannot sin, because he is born of God." The Christian is the one who is "born of God" and the Bible states clearly that such a one "doth not commit sin." According to the verse, the reason a Christian does not commit sin is because there is a "seed" that "remains in him" and therefore "he cannot sin, because he is born of God." The Bible indicates the "seed" refers to God's seed, and that this seed specifically is the "word of God" (Luke 8:11), by which believing sinners are "born again" (1 Peter 1:23), and this seed is "incorruptible" (incapable of being corrupted; i.e., sinless, and "cannot sin").

Since Christians have two natures, the old, sinful, Adamic one, and the new, sinless, Christian one, it is my belief that 1 John 3:9 is speaking of the Christian's new nature, the spiritual part of man that has been born again of the Spirit (John 3:5, 7, 8) and by the word of God (1 Peter 1:23), when the sinner places his or her faith in Christ for salvation (1 John 5:1, 4, 5; Luke 8:12). Technically, the Christian does not and cannot commit sin because the new nature within him does not. That is what this verse is talking about, and not eradication of the sinful nature.

Now some would quote 1 John 3:4, which states that, "Whosoever committeth sin transgresseth also the law: for sin is the transgression of the law," and substitute the word *commit* with *practice* to try and prove that the Christian no longer "practices" sin. But as the last half 1 John 3:4 shows, it is not the practice of sin that is considered the transgression of the law but the breaking of the law. As a matter of fact, James 2:10 says that if a person violates just *one point* of the law, then that person is guilty of transgressing *the whole law*. The reason for altering the reading is a well-intended but misguided attempt to defend the doctrine of eternal security against the Arminian who points an accusatory finger at a backslidden church member who personifies the "once saved, always saved" license to sin attitude. In his effort to refute the Arminian's charge, the eternal security advocate contends that "real" Christians can sin and still be saved, and not lose their salvation, as long as they sin occasionally and not on a regular basis, and so changes the word *commit* to *practice*.

As the verse stands, and as misunderstood as it is, it *seems* to plainly say that a person who commits sin is not a Christian, so the average Bible teacher tries to explain away the difficulty of 1 John 3:9 by "going to the Greek." But the common sense explanation in the preceding paragraphs precludes the necessity of changing the Book to accommodate anyone's theology or "practice." Instead of making the Book fit one's accepted theology, what is needed is to mold one's theology to fit the Bible.

[Generally speaking, I believe that a professing Christian ought not to "practice sin" (i.e., live a life that is characterized by consistent non-Christian behavior), and that if one does, they should examine their conversion experience. But the Book does not need to be altered or corrected to come to this conclusion.]

# SONS IN THE FAMILY

*For ye are all the children of God by faith in Christ Jesus.*

—GALATIANS 3:26

The Bible calls those who are believers in Christ "sons" in the family of God. In the Bible, 1 John 3:1–2 says, "Behold, what manner of love the Father hath bestowed upon us, that we should be called the sons of God. ... Beloved, now are we the sons of God."

Every Christian is a child of God by faith in the Lord Jesus Christ as Savior. (Galatians 3:26)

The old argument of the lost liberal religionist is that God would not send His children to hell any more than a good human father would place his children in an oven as punishment. But what they fail to recognize or admit is that their analogy is based upon a false premise. It assumes that the erroneous, liberal religious doctrine known as "the fatherhood of God and the brotherhood of man" is true, which asserts that God is the father of all mankind, and therefore all men are brothers in the family of God. But the Scriptures are clear that God is *not* the father of all mankind in the *spiritual* sense: the unsaved are *not* the children of God, and God is *not* their father. Only born-again believers are the children of God, and God is only the Father of those who have been born again. Jesus Christ was very clear when he told the lost Jews that God was not their Father, but the Devil was. In the eighth chapter of the Gospel of John, the unsaved Jews claimed they had "one Father, even God" (verse 41), but "Jesus said unto them, *If* God were your Father, ye would love me," which definitely implies that Jesus did *not* believe them to be the children of God (verse 42). And to further press the point, he also told them in the same breath, "Ye are of your father the devil" (verse 44). The unsaved are "children of disobedience" and "children of wrath" (Ephesians 2:2; 5:6; 2:3) and "children of the devil" (1 John 3:10).

The liberal religionist thinks the idea obscene that God would sentence His own children to hell, and rightly so (I would agree with them on this point, noting of course the distinction made in the previous paragraph regarding their false assumption); yet those who believe that a Christian can lose salvation believe akin to this very thing, that God the Father *would* consign His own children to the eternal flames of hell along with the unsaved children of Satan, thus making a monster out of the Bible's God of love. Such a notion is totally absurd. It's clear to see that the lost world of unregenerate mankind aren't God's children, and seems just as clear that God does not and will not condemn His children, saved by His grace, to hell.

The reader needs to understand that God *does* chasten His children, but he does *not* condemn them with the world. In the

Bible, 1 Corinthians 11:32 quite clearly says, "But when we (*the saved, children of God*) are judged, we are chastened (*disciplined, because we are God's children [Hebrews 12:7, 8]*) of the Lord, that we should not be condemned (*lose salvation and ultimately go to Hell*) with the world." Dr. John R. Rice wrote, "God punishes His children when they sin, but they are His children still."[45] God will discipline His disobedient sons and daughters, but He will never disown them.

Because Christians are in the family of God, they can never be lost. The saved are children of God by virtue of regeneration (a "new relation") and adoption (a "new position"). For a Christian to "lose salvation," they would have to become "un-born again" and God the Father would have to "un-adopt" some of His children. This chapter will examine these two doctrines in their relation to the doctrine of eternal security.

## A NEW RELATION: CHRISTIANS ARE SONS IN THE FAMILY OF GOD BY REGENERATION

The primary passage of Scripture regarding the new birth is found in John chapter 3, verses 1 through 18, where the Bible records the conversation between Nicodemus, an unsaved Jewish religious leader, and the Lord Jesus Christ, whom Nicodemus admits all agree is a "teacher come from God" (John 3:1, 2).

Through regeneration, a sinner is *made* a child of God through a supernatural, spiritual, second birth. Regeneration is what is referred to as the new birth and is known as being "born again."

A person is born again by the operation of the Spirit of God (John 3:6, 8) and by the agency of the word of God (1 Peter 1:23). This new birth is experienced by those who "believe on his name" and have "received him" as personal Savior (John 1:12). The born-again Christian is a "son of God" because he has been "born of God" (John 1:13) and "born of the Spirit" (John 3:6, 8), and shares God's very life by having become a "partaker of the divine nature" (2 Peter 1:4). This new birth is not the result of human descent ("of blood"), human determination ("of the will of the flesh"), or human design ("of the will of man"), but is "of God" (John 1:13). The new birth is an internal change that takes place inside the believing sinner that makes him a "new creature" in Christ (2 Corinthians 5:17). [This, by the way, is one of the major differences between biblical salvation and every other religious experience in the world. When a person gets saved, something happens to them on the inside. When a person joins a church or converts to a religion, nothing takes place on the inside; there is no internal change.]

When God created man and placed him in the Garden of Eden (Genesis 1–2), man died spiritually when he sinned and disobeyed God's command not to eat from the tree of the knowledge of good and evil (Genesis 1:26, 27; 3:1–6). The result of this was that all of Adam's descendants were thereafter born spiritually dead in their sins (Ephesians 2:1), separated from God because of their inherited, sinful, Adamic nature, and sentenced to physical and eternal death because of their sins (Romans 5:12). Every child of Adam faces the prospect of eternal separation from God and the "second death" in an everlasting lake of fire (Revelation 20:15; 21:8). The only remedy for this is spiritual renewal, which is accomplished in the repentant, believing sinner by the new birth when he receives Christ as Savior. The Lord Jesus said that those who are born again are "born of the Spirit" (John 3:6, 8).

There are two points to be made in relation to the new birth and eternal security.

First of all, if one will look at the second question that Nicodemus asked Jesus in John 3, there is a thought that comes to mind to those who actually meditate upon the Scriptures. Nicodemus asked, "How can a man be born when he is old? Can he enter the second time into his mother's womb, and be born?" (verse 4) The obvious answer is no. In the physical realm, it's impossible for a person to go back in time and become "unborn." If in the natural world it isn't possible to be "unborn," surely in the spiritual world (the "kingdom of God" [verse 3, 5]) it would be just as unreasonable to assume that a child of God could somehow become "*un*born-again."

Second, the apostle Peter writes in 1 Peter 3:3–5, 9, "Blessed be the God and Father of our Lord Jesus Christ, which according to his abundant mercy hath *begotten us again* unto a lively hope by the resurrection of Jesus Christ from the dead, To an inheritance incorruptible, and undefiled, and that fadeth not away, reserved in heaven for you, Who are kept by the power of God through faith unto salvation ready to be revealed in the last time ... *r*eceiving the end of your faith, even the salvation of your souls."

Simon Peter addresses these words of hope and encouragement to those who have been born again, for he includes himself among those whom God has "begotten ... again" (verse 3). He says the born-again believer has been promised an incorruptible, undefiled, permanent inheritance that is "reserved in heaven" for the children of God. For the Christian to lose his inheritance in heaven, he would have to lose his reservation. Since the reservation has been paid for by the precious blood of Christ (1 Peter 1:18, 19) and made in the believer's name, either God or the

Christian would have to "cancel" those reservations in order for that person to lose salvation. I contend that such a thing would never happen because not only is a place in heaven reserved for God's children, but also the Christian is "kept by the power of God" (verse 5). The word *kept* is similar to the word *reserved*; they mean in essence the same thing. When a person "reserves" a room, the hotel clerk "keeps" the room, or "holds" the room for the traveler. God has "reserved" His children's mansions in glory (John 14:2, 3), and God also "keeps" the Christian so that he will make it to his destination, which is heaven.

Those who disagree with the doctrine of eternal security would be quick to point out that Christians are "kept by the power of God *through faith*" (verse 5) and that the "end of your faith" means that Christians must persevere and "endure to the end" of their earthly lives in order to finally receive the "salvation of [their] souls" (verse 9). The answer to that objection is found in two places, particularly. In Hebrews 10:38, 39, the word of God says, "Now the just shall live by faith: but if any man draw back (*from living by faith; to stop believing*), my soul shall have no pleasure in him. But we are not of them who draw back unto perdition (*a lost condition; unsaved state*); but of them that believe to the saving of the soul." I join the writer of Hebrews in saying that I am also "of them that believe to the saving of the soul." And, hypothetically speaking, even if the Christian did stop believing, and drew back from faith, the Bible still says that "if we believe not, yet he abideth faithful: he cannot deny himself" (2 Timothy 2:13). [The reader is referred to Appendix 1—"Believeth or Believed?"]

Dr. Ironside sums up the argument very succinctly: "When we speak of the eternal security of the believer, what do we mean? We mean that once a poor sinner has been regenerated by the Word and the Spirit of God, once he has received a new life and a new nature, has been made partaker of the divine nature, once he has been justified from every charge before the throne of God, it is absolutely impossible that that man should ever again be a lost soul."[46]

## A NEW POSITION: CHRISTIANS ARE SONS IN THE FAMILY OF GOD BY ADOPTION

The doctrine of adoption is closely related to that of regeneration. Although these doctrines are similar, in that both have to do with the children of God's relationship to their heavenly Father, there are distinct differences.

C. I. Scofield says, "Adoption (*huiothesia*, 'placing of a son') is not so much a word of *relationship* as of *position*. The believer's relation to God as a child results from the new birth (John 1:12, 13), whereas adoption is the act of God whereby one already a child is, through redemption from the law, placed in the position of an adult son (Galatians 4:1–5). The indwelling Spirit gives the realization of this in the believer's present experience (Galatians 4:6); but the full manifestation of the believer's sonship awaits the resurrection, change, and translation of saints, which is called 'the redemption of the body' (Romans 8:23; 1 Thessalonians 4:14–17; Ephesians 1:14; 1 John 3:2)."[47] This resurrection and redemption of the body occurs at the event on God's prophetic calendar known as the "rapture" of the church.

A good summary of the doctrine of adoption is written by William Evans in his classic book on theology *The Great Doctrines of the Bible*: "Regeneration begins the new life. ... Adoption admits man into the family of God with filial joy. Regeneration has to do with our change in nature … adoption, with our change in position. In regeneration the believer becomes a child of God (John 1:12, 13); in adoption, the believer, already a child, receives a place as an adult son; thus the child becomes a son, the minor becomes an adult (Galatians 4:1–7)."[48] He explains the meaning of adoption as *"the placing of a son.* It is a legal metaphor as regeneration is a physical one. It is a Roman word, for adoption was hardly, if at all, known among the Jews. It means the taking by one man of the son of another to be his son, so that that son has the same position and all the advantages of a son by birth."[49]

As pointed out by Mr. Evans, the word (*adoption*) is used only by the apostle Paul, and then in reference to the Christian "when questions of rights, privileges, and heirship are involved (Galatians 4:5; Romans 8:15, 23; 9:4; Ephesians 1:5)."[50]

Through adoption, a saved sinner, already a born-again child of God, is *placed* as an adult son in the family, and blessed with the privileges and assumes the responsibilities that attend such a position. Some of the evidences of adoption are the following:

- Christians "are led by the Spirit." (Romans 8:14; Galatians 5:18)
- They "have a childlike confidence in God." (Galatians 4:5, 6)
- They "have liberty of access to the Father." (Ephesians 3:12)
- They "have love for the brethren." (1 John 2:9–11; 5:1)
- They "are obedient." (1 John 5:1–3)[51]

In the Roman world adoption was a significant and common practice. A man was expected to pass his wealth on to his son(s). If a man had no sons, he would have to adopt someone who would make a worthy son. These adoptions were not infant adoptions as is common today. Older boys and adult men were normally adopted. In some cases, the adoptee might even be older than the man who was adopting him. When the adoption was legally approved, the adoptee would have all his debts cancelled and he would receive a new name. He would be the legal son of his adoptive father and entitled to all the rights and benefits of a son. A father could disown his natural-born son, but an adoption was irreversible.

When we come to faith in Christ all our debts are cancelled (1 John 2:12 — our sins are forgiven), we are given a new name (Revelation 2:17), and we are given all the rights and privileges belonging to the heirs of God (Romans 8:15-17).

A wonderful illustration of our adoption by the heavenly Father into His family is found in the book Ben-Hur: A Tale of the Christ by Lew Wallace, and in the movie starring Charlton Heston. In it we see a vivid portrayal of Roman adoption. In the movie, Judah Ben-Hur (a Jew) has been imprisoned on a Roman galley ship as a rower. When the ship sinks in battle, Judah escapes and saves the life of a Roman commander named Arrius. Arrius's only son has been killed, and he ultimately adopts Judah, who is pardoned for his supposed crimes. He is also given a new name, "young Arrius," and has all the rights of inheritance. In the scene where the adoption is announced, Arrius takes off his ancestral signet ring and gives it to young Arrius. As young Arrius takes the ring and places it on his finger, he says what we as the adopted children of God can say: "I have received a new life, a new home, and a new Father." What a blessing that is to know![52]

In the book of Ephesians 1:4–6, the Bible says, "According as he hath chosen us in him before the foundation of the world, that we should be holy and without blame before him in love: Having predestinated us unto the adoption of children by Jesus Christ to himself, according to the good pleasure of his will, To the praise of the glory of his grace, wherein he hath made us accepted in the beloved."

Any and all saved people were chosen by God before the foundation of the world "in him;" that is, "in Christ." According to 1 Peter 1:2, God's choosing to salvation is based on His "foreknowledge" (i.e., the knowledge He had of who would trust the Lord Jesus Christ for their salvation). In other words, God chose in eternity past those who would be saved because He knew those who would *choose* His Son as Savior in their lifetime.

The ones who are "predestinated ... unto the adoption of children" are identified as "us" (i.e., those who were chosen in Christ, the already saved). In other words, to be predestinated one must already be saved. Predestination has to do with believers wherever you find the word in the New Testament. In this case, Christians are being placed as sons (adoption) in the family because they are already in the family by birth (regeneration). And this is all "according to the good pleasure of his will, To the praise of the glory of his grace, wherein he hath made us accepted in the beloved" (Ephesians 1:6).

(The Bible student should of course understand that salvation is an instantaneous act—at the moment of faith in Christ; and that the different aspects of salvation are simultaneous acts that occur at the moment of salvation [those aspects of salvation being, particularly, regeneration and adoption under the current discussion; but also justification, sanctification, remission, redemption, reconciliation, et al.])

Having been adopted (placed as a son in the family), some of the blessings and privileges that attend such a position are that Christians become the "objects of God's peculiar love (John 17:23), and His fatherly care (Luke 12:27–33). We have the family name (1 John 3:1; Ephesians 3:14, 15), the family likeness (Romans 8:29); family love (John 13:35; 1 John 3:14); a filial spirit (Romans 8:15; Galatians 4:6); a family service (John 14:23, 24; 15:8). We receive fatherly chastisement (Hebrews 12:5–11); fatherly comfort (Isaiah 66:13; 2 Corinthians 1:4), and an inheritance (1 Peter 1:3–5; Romans 8:17)."[53]

Although it is true that believers are adopted "by Jesus Christ unto [God the Father] himself" (Ephesians 1:5) at the moment of salvation, that is only part of the adoption process. The soul and spirit have been saved, but the body as of yet has not. It is still the same old flesh, possessed of a sinful nature, which is headed for the grave. But one day all Christians, both the quick and the dead, will receive new bodies. St. Paul wrote, "We ourselves groan within ourselves, waiting for the adoption, to wit, the redemption of our body" (Romans 8:23). This will occur at the rapture of the church, when Jesus comes back with the souls of the saved, to reunite them with their glorified bodies, and to make them "like unto His glorious body" (Philippians 3:20–21). The adoption process will then be complete.

So for the time being, the world does not really know Christians for who they are. The adopted children of God are for the moment *incognito*, but one day the world will see born-again believers for whom they really are. "Beloved, now are we the sons of God, and *it doth not yet appear what we shall be*: but we know that, when he shall appear, *we shall be like him*; for we shall see him as he is" (1 John 3:2). Paul the apostle said something similar to this in Romans 8:18, in the same context of adoption: "For I reckon that the sufferings of this present time are not worthy to be compared with the glory which shall be *revealed* in us" when the sons of God are manifested. What a day that will be!

With as much as the Father has invested in the Christian, it would seem implausible that God would disown those whom He has taken the trouble to adopt. In Western society, adoption is a long, tedious, expensive, time-consuming, and many times frustrating, process. It's a legal affair that establishes a relationship that's more binding than biological birth. Being that is so, it would only be logical to conclude that since Christians are God's children by birth, and moreover by adoption also, that for a child of God to be lost again, the legal proceedings of adoption would have to be reversed by the court of heaven. It stretches credulity to believe that God would "un-adopt" one of His children that His only begotten Son died to save. The old adage is true: "Once a son, always a son."

For the child of God to be lost after he has been saved, he would have to be "un-born again" and "un-adopted." Such will never be the case for any Christian, for Jesus said in John 6:39, "And this is the Father's will which hath sent me, that of all which he hath given me *I should lose nothing*, but should raise it up again at the last day." The Lord Jesus Christ won't refuse any who come to Him by faith (John 6:37), and He just as certainly is not going to "lose" any of the children that the Father has given Him. Christians are, therefore, eternally safe and secure.

# THE SCRIPTURES SAY SO

*If we receive the witness of men, the witness of God
is greater: for this is the witness of God which he
hath testified of his Son. He that believeth on the
Son of God hath the witness in himself: he that
believeth not God hath made him a liar; because
he believeth not the record that God gave of his Son.
And this is the record, that God hath given to us
eternal life, and this life is in his Son. He that hath
the Son hath life; and he that hath not the Son of
God hath not life. These things have I written unto
you that believe on the name of the Son of God; that
ye may know that ye have eternal life, and that ye
may believe on the name of the Son of God.*
—1 JOHN 5:9–13

The scriptural proof that has been presented thus far leads
me to simply say that eternal security is true because the
scriptures say so. It has been shown from the Scriptures that the

preponderance of evidence weighs in favor of the Christian's eternal security. The sound arguments offered in this treatise ought to compel any unbiased student of the Scriptures to agree that the doctrine of eternal security is an indisputable biblical truth.

From the study of the word of God, it can be clearly seen that the Lord's salvation is a present possession, a perpetual reality, a purchased gift, and a promise of God.

## SALVATION IS A PRESENT POSSESSION

The Scriptures unmistakably declare that the believer in Christ has eternal life. In 1 John 5:11, the Bible states that God has "given to us [Christians] eternal life." Verse 12 declares that those who have the Son [Christians] have life. Verse 13 plainly affirms that Christians "have eternal life."

Comparing scripture with scripture reinforces the idea that eternal life is the present possession of all born-again believers. The apostle John stressed throughout his Gospel that those who "believe" in Christ have eternal life as a present possession. In John 3:16, he quotes Jesus Christ as saying, "For God so loved the world, that he gave his only begotten Son, that whosoever believeth in him should not perish, but *have everlasting life.*" In John 3:36, he quotes John the Baptist as saying, "He that believeth on the Son *hath everlasting life.*" And in John 5:24 he quotes Jesus again, saying, "Verily, verily, I say unto you, He that heareth my word, and believeth on him that sent me, *hath everlasting life.*"

What a blessing it is for the Christian to know that he has eternal life as a present possession!

# SALVATION IS A PERPETUAL REALITY

Not only is it clear that Christians have eternal life as a present possession, but it is also just as clear that Christians who have eternal life have it as a permanent possession; therefore, salvation is a perpetual reality. The salvation they *obtained* through faith in Jesus Christ is also *retained* because of the Christ in whom their faith resides.

One can know that salvation is a perpetual reality by virtue of the very nature of the life that the believer possesses (i.e., this life is *eternal* and *everlasting*). Numerous verses attest to this. Just a few examples should suffice. *"Everlasting* life" is found in John 3:16, John 3:36, and John 5:24. *"Eternal* life" is found in John 10:28, Romans 6:23, and 1 John 5:13. *Everlasting* life is life that never ends. *Eternal* life is life that has no beginning and no end. *Eternal* life encompasses eternity past and future. Being that it is eternal, it is timeless.

God said in Isaiah 51:6, "My salvation shall be for ever, and my righteousness shall not be abolished." God's salvation is eternal and "shall be for ever." So it follows that those who have received God's salvation (Psalm 51:12 — "thy salvation") are saved "for ever" because His salvation is "for ever." One preacher put it this way: "If I am saved then I will live as long as God lives." Since God is eternal, then the salvation He bestows upon believers is eternal, and the believer is eternally secure.

Other familiar scriptures that attest to the eternal security of the Christian are John 10:28, where Jesus said His sheep "shall never perish," and John 5:24, where Jesus said that believers "shall not come into condemnation" but are "passed from death unto life." The apostle Paul was "persuaded" in 2 Timothy 1:12 that the Lord Jesus would "keep" his soul until His return, and in Romans 8:38–39 stated emphatically that he was "persuaded, that neither death, nor life, nor angels, nor principalities, nor powers, nor things present, nor things to come, Nor height, nor depth, nor any other creature, shall be able to separate us from the love of God, which is in Christ Jesus our Lord." The Christian's salvation *is* a perpetual reality.

## SALVATION IS A PURCHASED GIFT

One of the many great verses in the Bible is Romans 6:23. The word of God there says, "For the wages of sin is death; but the gift of God is eternal life through Jesus Christ our Lord." This verse of scripture contains both a negative and a positive truth. Negatively, it speaks of the "bad news" of sin and its penalty—death. Conversely, it speaks of the positive aspect, the "good news"—that God offers the gift of eternal life to the world through His Son, Jesus Christ. The Bible here clearly says that eternal life is the gift of God. Also, in Ephesians 2:8, Paul reiterates that salvation is the "gift of God."

The apostle John corroborates the apostle Paul when he writes in 1 John 5:10–12 that eternal life is a gift of God, given to Christians. He writes that those who have believed the record that God gave of His Son (verse 10), who have received the Son (verse 12), and have believed on the Son of God (verse 13) to the saving of their souls, "have eternal life."

As with any gift, eternal life is a gift that was purchased by God in order to give to those whom He loves and wants to bless. The "gift of God" is the gift of eternal life that was bought and paid for by God Himself when Jesus died on the cross and shed His precious blood. (Acts 20:28; Hebrews 9:12, 14; 1 Peter 1:18, 19)

This gift of God is offered to all, but it is only and actually *given* to those who believe the Gospel of Christ and have received the Christ of the Gospel as their personal Savior. (John 1:12, 13; 5:24; 10:28)

## SALVATION IS A PROMISE OF GOD

God did not write in the sky to assure any individual that he is saved, but He recorded it in the Scriptures, which is far better and more trustworthy. The Bible says that the Christian has a "more sure word of prophecy" than the literal voice of God from heaven (2 Peter 1:19). This scripture evidently teaches that: "A verse (of scripture) is better than a vision (in the sky) or a voice (from heaven)."

The apostle Paul speaks of the "hope of eternal life, which God, that cannot lie, *promised* before the world began" (Tit. 1:2). The apostle John states emphatically, "And this is the *promise* that he hath *promised* us, even eternal life" (1 John 2:25). One of the most familiar, well-beloved and oft-used verses in the Holy Bible that speaks to this subject is 1 John 5:13, which reads: "These things have I written unto you that believe on the name of the Son of God; that ye may know that ye have eternal life." What a promise the Christian has in the word of God! Jesus said "the scripture cannot be broken" (John 10:35). God does not break His promises. The child of God can know that he has eternal life because God has promised it in His word.

Jesus said that He will never "cast out" (reject) a true believer. The exact quote is "Him that cometh to me I will *in no wise* ['not in any degree, way, or under any condition'] cast out" (John 6:37). Jesus will never allow a true believer to perish; He said, "I give unto them [believers] eternal life, and they [believers] shall never perish" (John 10:28).

The Lord Jesus will never "forsake" (renounce) a true believer (Hebrews 13:5). While dining at a Hardee's restaurant outside of Eglin Air Force Base back in 1979, I sat with an elderly gentleman whom I had just met. He'd asked to sit with me as there were no empty tables available. As we were talking, I asked him if he were a Christian, and he said he was. I asked him where he went to church, and he said he was a lifelong Methodist. I then asked him if he were to die did he know for sure he would go to heaven. Of that, he said he was not sure, even though he professed to have faith in Christ. We discussed eternal security. As a Methodist, he said he had been saved but believed that a Christian could lose his salvation if he turned away from following Christ. A verse came to my mind, and I quoted to him Hebrews 13:5, where Jesus said, "I will never leave thee, nor forsake thee."

The gentleman said, "Yes, but you can leave Christ."

I replied, "But the verse says He will never leave you. So if you tried to leave Christ, you really couldn't get away from Him, because He said He would never leave you." The expression on his face revealed that a light came on in his soul. Then he said, "I never thought of it that way." Whether he remained convinced after we parted company, I don't know. But for that moment, he was visibly moved and blessed by the truth he had just seen for the first time.

The fact that God would not renege on His promise of eternal life is verified in Romans 11:29, where the Bible says, "The gifts and calling of God are without repentance." The word *gift* can be applied to the gift of eternal life (Romans 6:23); the word *calling* can be applied to the call to salvation that has been extended to lost humanity and answered by those who have responded in faith to that call and received Christ as Savior (Romans 8:30; 1 Corinthians 1:9); and the phrase "without repentance" means that the Lord will never change His mind, reverse His decision, and recall the salvation of a genuine Christian by "taking back" the gift of eternal life from a repentant, believing sinner. He will completely and eventually save every sinner who has received His Son as their personal Savior.

In his discussion of the Old Testament patriarch Jacob's faith and failures in his commentary *Gleanings in Genesis,* Arthur W. Pink considers eternal security. He asks if it were possible that Jacob fell from grace and lost his salvation due to his actions after his professed belief in the Lord God. Pink answers, "Surely not ... we must reject any such suggestion, for the Scriptures are plain and explicit on the point that one who has been born again cannot be unborn —an unfaithful and unworthy child of God I may be, but I am still *His child*, nevertheless. The gifts and calling of God are 'without repentance'—without *change of mind* (Romans 11:29). Once a sinner has been called out of darkness into God's marvelous light, and once God has given to him light and salvation, he never undoes that calling or withdraws His gift, for the sinner did nothing whatever of himself to *merit* God's gift, and he can do nothing to *demerit* it." [54]

Dr J. Dwight Pentecost, in his book Things Which Become Sound Doctrine, writes about the subject of salvation and the believer's eternal security. In it he asserts that: "The promise of God is a basis for our [eternal] security. We go into a familiar passage such as John 3:16 where it is made so clear: '...God so loved the world, that he gave his only begotten Son, that whosoever believeth in him should not perish, but have everlasting life.' Notice the two aspects of the promise: negatively, he shall not perish; positively, he shall have everlasting life! When God offers a man life, God offers a man only one kind of life, and that is eternal life. Eternal life is the life of God, and as God's life could never be terminated by death, so the life of God, given to the child of God, could never be terminated. We submit to you that the promise of God to give eternal life to the one who accepts Christ as his Savior is a sufficient basis for our [eternal] security."

It is plain to see from the word of God that Biblical salvation is a present possession, a perpetual reality, a purchased gift, and a promise of God.

# THE SURENESS OF SALVATION

*Who shall separate us from the love of Christ?
shall tribulation, or distress, or persecution, or
famine, or nakedness, or peril, or sword? As it
is written, For thy sake we are killed all the day
long; we are accounted as sheep for the slaughter.
Nay, in all these things we are more than
conquerors through him that loved us. For I am
persuaded, that neither death, nor life, nor angels,
nor principalities, nor powers, nor things present,
nor things to come, Nor height, nor depth, nor any
other creature, shall be able to separate us from the
love of God, which is in Christ Jesus our Lord.*
— ROMANS 8:35–39

*For the which cause I also suffer these things:
nevertheless I am not ashamed: for I know whom
I have believed, and am persuaded that he is able
to keep that which I have committed unto him
against that day.*
— 2 TIMOTHY 1:12

In the verses quoted above, the apostle Paul declares his confidence in the keeping ability of the Savior. He was "persuaded" that the Lord would keep his soul, and that he would eventually be saved in the end. Paul had no worries about "losing" salvation, but was *totally convinced* of his security in Christ. Paul was sure of his salvation. This is also known as having *assurance* of salvation.

Christians are saved for time and for eternity: *once saved*, a child of God is *always saved*. Believers in the Lord Jesus Christ do not have a "may-be" or a "hope-so" kind of salvation, but a "know-so" salvation. The Bible informs its readers that a person can "know" that they are saved (see 1 John 5:13).

Dr. Ryrie explains that *"[a]ssurance concerns the realization that a person has eternal life.* But security is a true fact whether or not an individual has assurance of that or not"[55] and that *"[a]ssurance is the confident realization that one has eternal life.* Security is a biblical truth whether or not one has assurance."[56] (Italics added)

Is it possible to doubt one's salvation? Is it conceivable for a Christian to be saved, safe and secure, *yet not sure* that they are? The answer is yes. After a person has been saved for a time, they may discover that there is a difference between salvation and assurance; between being saved and being sure of it. There are some Christians who may "doubt their salvation" and "question their conversion." I have come across those who have been saved but were not sure. They lacked the assurance of their salvation. Any Christian will easily confess, "Yes, I have accepted Christ as my Savior," but there are some who cannot bring themselves to say, "Yes, I have accepted Christ as my Savior, *and I know* that I am saved and going to heaven when I die."

Personally, I was saved one night at my bedside, but within one week, doubts began to trouble me. Later, as I grew in the grace, knowledge, and doctrines of the Lord, I received the assurance of my salvation.

Christians should understand that it isn't uncommon to have doubts. Even the greatest of all the prophets, John the Baptist, had doubts concerning the Lord Jesus Christ (Matthew 11:3), but the Lord did not condemn him—He complimented him and encouraged his faith.

In Matthew 14:22–33, the disciples were out on the Sea of Galilee during a fearsome storm. They were not sure if they were going to make it through and survive the tempest. Jesus spoke to them and asked, "O thou of little faith, wherefore didst thou doubt?" Then He spoke words of hope and encouragement and assurance: "Be of good cheer: it is I; be not afraid," and then He calmed the raging sea.

What a wonderful illustration of security and assurance. The disciples were doubting if they would make it to the other side because of the overwhelming circumstances that surrounded them, even to the point of questioning if Jesus Himself cared and was concerned enough to deliver them. Yet in spite of their doubts and fears, Jesus got them to the other side, safe and sound. Even so, every Christian is on board the old ship of Zion (a figurative expression for the Church of God), out on the sea of Time, sailing towards Eternity. The storms of life may beat and batter the children of God, and at times doubts and confusion may arise, but Jesus Christ the Savior will see to it that all His disciples safely land on Heaven's shore.

When someone doubts their salvation there are two possible explanations: the individual really *is* lost and needs to be saved, or the person doubting simply lacks assurance. That is why the word of God admonishes the readers of its sacred pages to "make [their] calling and election sure" and to "examine [themselves], whether [they] be in the faith" or not (2 Peter 1:10. 11; 2 Corinthians 13:5).

Near the Texas/Louisiana border, there's a little town (population 150) named *Uncertain*. Imagine asking someone who lived there, "Where do you live?" and they answered, "Uncertain." Puzzled, you follow up with another question: "You mean you aren't certain where you live?" And they replied: "I'm certain I live in Uncertain." The Christian who doubts their salvation is sure of one thing: they're certain they live in uncertainty; they're sure they aren't sure!

## SOME CONSEQUENCES OF DOUBTING ONE'S SALVATION

The person who doubts will be like those described in Deuteronomy 28:66, 67: "Thy life shall hang in doubt before thee; and thou shalt fear day and night, and shalt have none assurance of thy life: In the morning thou shalt say, Would God it were even! and at even thou shalt say, Would God it were morning! for the fear of thine heart wherewith thou shalt fear." Fear and anxiety will haunt those who stand in doubt of their salvation.

One consequence of doubt is that a Christian will lose the joy of salvation. King David asked God in Psalm 51:12 to "restore" the "joy" of His "salvation." The salvation of the Lord is a joyous thing, "Wherein ye greatly rejoice" (1 Peter 1:6). But if one doubts whether they are saved or not, it is difficult, if not impossible, to maintain that joy. It is hard to be happy in Jesus when one is not sure they are in His favor and are uncertain of their salvation. (And being that "the joy of the LORD is your strength" [Nehemiah 8:10], the doubting believer will be weak in faith.)

Many Christian hymns speak of the believer's assurance of salvation and certainty of heaven, but it would be difficult to sing about going to heaven when one's own eternal destination is in question. (One of the funniest things to me is meeting those who believe they can lose their salvation and find that their favorite hymn is "Blessed Assurance.") Without eternal security and the assurance of salvation, many a professing Christian goes through life with the constant fear of losing their salvation and being lost eternally. Brethren, these things ought not to be so.

The assurance of salvation and the joy of the Lord go hand in hand. They are Siamese twins, and there's no having the one without having the other. The apostle John wrote his first epistle so that a Christian's "joy may be full" (1 John 1:4), and one of the great emphases is on the subject of a believer being able to assert that he is saved, in possession of eternal life, and *knows* it. The little word *know* appears twenty-two times in the 105 verses that make up the short book of First John—that's once for every five verses! It is apparent that John wanted his readers to know certain truths, one of them being the sureness of the Christian's personal salvation.

Another consequence of doubt is that a Christian will lose the motive for service. The child of God knows that works do not save or merit eternal life; therefore, the Christian works for Christ because he is saved, not in order to become saved. A Christian is motivated to work for Christ because he is saved, not to merit salvation. The believer has been saved "unto good works" (Ephesians 2:10) and understands that living for Christ is simply "reasonable service" (Romans 12:1, 2). The true believer who lacks assurance finds himself in a genuine dilemma. It causes a person to wonder: "Am I truly doing this service for

God? Or am I trying to impress the Lord that I am saved, when I'm not sure, instead of doing my best to please the Lord because I know that I am saved?"

So, not being sure of their salvation, Christian service may come to a halt in such a person's life, because, lacking assurance, they are discouraged, and therefore have no motivation to be busy about the Lord's work. It will limit their effectiveness for the Lord and their usefulness in the Church. (In some cases, such Christians may find themselves performing Christian service in order to "prove" to themselves that they are saved, and instead of working *from* salvation, in reality they begin working *for* salvation, which confuses the issue that much more for those who know that works do not earn salvation. It is a vicious cycle that can result in years of fear and frustration.) The famous American evangelist D. L. Moody said, "I have never known a Christian who was any good in the work of Christ who did not have assurance of salvation."

There is an interesting story told about the Golden Gate Bridge. Allegedly during the first phase of its construction, no safety devices were used, and twenty-three men fell to their deaths in the San Francisco Bay. Needless to say, production went down.[57] The engineer who envisioned the bridge and was head of the project, Joseph B. Strauss, was also a pioneer in construction safety. "He was the first to require hard hats and daily sobriety tests for workers, and as a precaution, *a safety net below the entire bridge site*, which saved the lives of 19 men. They were known as members of the *Half-way To Hell Club* (isn't that interesting? It's good to know that some unsaved sinners actually still believe in Hell). Loss of life was minimal on the vast project ... making the Golden Gate Bridge construction one of the safest in history."[58]

Of those who fell after the safety net was installed, very few, if any, perished. The workers' production output increased by 25 percent—because the workers were sure they were safe! By the same token, you cannot put your all into serving God unless you have assurance of your soul's eternal safety in Christ. A Christian needs to have the assurance of eternal life to serve God more faithfully and without worry and doubt.

When it comes to soul-winning efforts, doubt will hinder evangelism. The church is commanded by Christ, compelled by the Spirit, and constrained by love to be witnesses for the Lord. But the specter of doubt chides and says, "How can you tell others about what you are not sure of yourself?" One must be convinced of and sure of his own salvation in order to be an effective witness for Christ.

There's a quaint story about a stranger who was asking a little boy for directions. The man asked, "How do you get to town?"

The boy said, "I don't know."

"Do you know where Route 15 is?"

"No, I don't know."

"Where does this road go?"

"I don't know."

"Do you know the name of this street?"

"No, I don't know."

"Do you know anything?"

"I know I ain't lost."

Although not a perfect analogy, the point is that it will be hard for any Christian to witness for the Lord with authority and win souls until they themselves know they "ain't lost."

And then another consequence of doubt is that the Christian loses the ability to resist evil. Christians who doubt their personal salvation will be plagued with worries and fears, unsure of being on God's side, or of God being on their side, and so will linger on the sidelines of the battle against worldliness and wickedness. The Christian who lacks assurance of salvation cannot successfully resist the world, the flesh, and the devil in their own life until the doubts are settled and there is personal assurance of salvation. The Christian who lacks assurance will be engaged in a losing battle and continually defeated by doubt.

## SOME CAUSES FOR DOUBTING ONE'S SALVATION

Why would someone doubt his or her salvation? That is a good question, even one that the Lord Jesus posed to His disciples in the example already mentioned. In Matthew 14:33 Jesus asked, "Wherefore [why] didst thou doubt?" Well, there are probably many reasons that cause a Christian to doubt, and following are some that I have dealt with throughout the course of my ministry.

Some doubt because they cannot remember the specific date, time, or place. Some folks can remember the *exact* date, time, and location they were saved, but some cannot pinpoint it specifically. Personally, I have always believed that I was saved and converted to Christ on Sunday, May 8, 1976, at eleven o'clock at night in my bedroom at home, while living in Hanford, California. But years later, I discovered that the actual date I was converted was May 11. Due to an apparently faulty memory, the date was off by three days according to my recollection. Nevertheless, the fact of my new birth was more important than knowing the exact date. I was and am saved, nonetheless. We should be thankful that the Lord Himself is the divine bookkeeper!

But assurance is not based on remembering specifically when and where you were converted, but upon knowing what one did—did the person receive Jesus Christ as personal Savior?

To say that a person is not saved because he cannot remember the *exact* time, date and place is like saying that a person really was not born into this world because they cannot remember the day. (My father and his stepfather were both born without having birth certificates. Neither one of them knew the dates of their birth, so they had to go by what they had been told by their families. But they are living proof that they were born!) Some people simply have poor memories as to details and do not remember the specifics. This may cause some to doubt their salvation experience. (This is why it is a good idea to annotate the time, date, and place of conversion in a new Christian's Bible, to preclude this from becoming a problem for them in the future.)

Some doubt because they did not have the "same experience" someone else had. Some folks have had spectacular conversion experiences and can describe their testimony in the most glowing terms and preach about their experience with great enthusiasm. If someone else did not have that same kind of experience, the devil may slip up beside such a vulnerable believer and say, "*You didn't get what they got.*"

The apostle Paul's conversion experience was unlike anyone else's in history: he was blinded by a light from heaven, thrown from his horse, and Jesus spoke to him audibly—none of that happened to anyone else in history, certainly not me, yet anyone who has trusted Christ as Savior is just as saved as Paul was!

Not everyone's conversion is a sensational story or a highly charged emotional experience. The Christian's assurance is not based on having the same experience as their favorite preacher or Christian hero. Each salvation experience is personal and unique to the individual child of God. The bottom line is that "[h]e that *believeth* on the Son hath everlasting life" (John 3:36).

Some doubt because they did not have the "same emotions" that someone else had. Following the idea of having the same experience, for some people, the conversion experience is a very *emotional* one, but it must be stressed and remembered that salvation and assurance is based upon faith, not feelings. Just the same, assurance of salvation must be founded upon one's faith, not their "feelings."

Different people express their emotions in different ways, unique to their personality: some smile, some shout, some cry, some lift their hands. Some express no outward emotion at all. Not everybody shouted, not everybody hugged his neighbor, and not everybody "swung from the rafters" as part of their salvation experience.

When I received Christ and was saved, I felt as if a weight had been lifted off my shoulders, as if my heart was being pumped full of hot, liquid love (to use Charles Finney's description of his experience, described in his *Autobiography*), as if it would literally explode and leap out of my chest. There was a feeling of being cleansed inwardly, as if God gave me "a bath on the inside." But no one should doubt their salvation because they didn't have the same emotions I had.

Here is a good illustration. If a married man or woman will remember when they were first married, they know that it was a unique, one-time experience that was followed by the honeymoon. Sometime after that, the routine of married life set in. How it felt to get married on their wedding day may not be the same feeling that is experienced years later. Whether there is a feeling or not, and whatever that feeling is, the fact is that the married couple is married, regardless of how it felt then or how it feels now. The fact of marriage is not based upon feelings or the lack of feelings. The same is true when it concerns one's personal salvation. (There was a time when every believer was unsaved, not married to Christ, and in a lost condition, and most of that time, there was no feeling of being lost or condemned, yet the fact is that it was true. Just as a lost man cannot base his condemnation on feeling, so a Christian cannot base his assurance on feeling.)

The great German reformer Martin Luther wrote why Christians should not trust in their feelings:

For feelings come and feelings go, And feelings are deceiving.
My warrant is the Word of God, Nothing
else is worth believing.
Though all my soul should feel condemned
For want of some sweet token,
There is One greater than my heart,
Whose word cannot be broken.
I'll stand on His unchanging word, Till soul and body sever,
For though all things should pass away,
His word shall stand forever.

A Christian's salvation and assurance does not depend on someone else's experience or feelings. Each individual Christian has their own, personal, and unique testimony of how they came to know the Savior, and each one is just as relevant as anyone else's. Everyone has their *own* salvation story.

# THE CURE FOR DOUBTING ONE'S SALVATION

The cure for doubting one's salvation is twofold.

First, there must be an examination of the evidence. This would be the *objective* ground of assurance, which is found in the Holy Bible, the written word of God. In fact, the apostle John says that he wrote his first epistle for this very purpose (1 John 5:13).

The scripture says in 2 Corinthians 13:5, "Examine yourselves, whether ye be in the faith; prove your own selves. Know ye not your own selves, how that Jesus Christ is in you, except ye be reprobates?" This verse admonishes the reader to perform a spiritual self-examination to determine whether or not he is truly "in the faith" (i.e., saved). And in the same verse, the Bible gives the acid test to determine whether one is saved or not. The word *prove* means to test. The word *reprobate* means "to *fail* the test." So, what is the true test of a believer? The answer is that Jesus Christ is "in you." When a person receives Christ as Savior, that person "takes" Him, "accepts" Him, and/or "admits" Him into their heart and life, and Jesus Christ enters the believer's body and is, literally, "in" the Christian, and, therefore, that individual can know they are saved because the "hope of glory" (i.e., the Christ of salvation) is now in them (Colossians 1:27; Revelation 3:20). Is the Lord Jesus Christ in you? If He is, then you can say that you are saved. If He is not in you, then you are not saved, because you have failed the test, and are therefore a "reprobate."

Secondly, there must be a confirmation of the experience. This would be the *subjective* ground of assurance, which is the Christian's actual experience. The refrain of an old-time gospel song says: "I was there when it happened, and I ought to know."[59] Not to cast doubt or contradict what has previously been discussed, but a good question is: "Does the doubting Christian have a recollection of a time and place in his life where he believes the Holy Spirit of God convicted his heart of sin and convinced him of the need for salvation? Was there a time when the doubter felt a need of God's forgiveness for his sins?" A former Bible professor, Dr. Peter Ruckman, said in a sermon, "A man will never get saved until he feels his need for forgiveness." The famous British evangelist George Whitefield in his sermon "The Method of Grace" said that a sinner will never get saved until he gets *sick of his sin.* Now, again, sinners are not saved by feelings, but the testimony of many Christian converts seems to indicate there are two feelings that are almost universal: (1) a feeling of guilt and the need of God's forgiveness *before* conversion, and (2) a feeling of relief, as if a literal burden was lifted from off their shoulders, *after* conversion. (Remember John Bunyan's character, Pilgrim, as described in his allegory *Pilgrim's Progress*, whose burden of sin rolled off his back when he knelt before the Cross.)

Now, if the doubter can identify a time and place when and where he believes he was converted and received the Lord Jesus as Savior, he needs to determine if there has been a change in his life since that time. The Bible tells us, "Therefore, if any man be in Christ, he is a new creature: old things are passed away; behold, all things are become new" (2 Corinthians 5:17). Next to the word of God, a changed life is the best evidence that a person has been born again, in that a holy life substantiates what the heart claims to believe. The professing Christian ought to have a love for the Lord, for the Bible, for the Church, for the brethren, and a desire to live a righteous and holy life. A genuine Christian will believe the word of God and should be impelled by the indwelling Spirit of God to conform his or her behavior to the will of God as revealed in the Bible. If the life is *not* right, there may be doubts about one's salvation; however, when the life and attitude is right, then the doubts will most likely go away if one is truly saved. (Refer back to my comments on 1 John 2:3.)

## MAINTAINING ASSURANCE BY REMAINING IN FELLOWSHIP WITH GOD

Once a person has established their relationship with God by being born again, they will want to maintain fellowship with their heavenly Father. Maintaining fellowship does not mean "staying saved." Once a person is saved, they are safe forever. They cannot lose their salvation; they cannot forfeit the salvation God has given them. As one preacher put it, man is "saved by grace, not by grease." The Christian need not be worried about slipping out of God's hand and going to hell. God will keep His children until the end and save them to the uttermost. (Hebrews 7:25)

One of the benefits of maintaining fellowship with the Lord is that it will contribute to one's assurance of salvation.

In 1 John chapter 1, verses 3–7, the context is not salvation, and it is not relationship. The context is *fellowship.* Fellowship, as one man said, is two fellows in the same boat getting along with each other. If one of them gets out of fellowship with the other one, then that is what is called "rocking the boat." Fellowship with God is "getting along with God" and enjoying His presence and blessing in one's life. When a Christian gets out of line with God, he is out of fellowship with Him, and that is what is called being "backslidden."

How can one maintain fellowship with God? How can a person enjoy His presence and blessing in their life as a Christian, including assurance of salvation? Notice two phrases the apostle John uses in his first epistle in reference to maintaining fellowship.

In 1 John 1: 7, observe the phrase, "if we walk in the light." A Christian must walk in the light of the Lord and His truth. Christians are supposed to behave like children of God. They are supposed to live the right kind of life. They are meant to live according to the Bible. In verse 6, the apostle John speaks of those who say they're in fellowship with God but walk in darkness. This is the kind of person who "says one thing and does another." This is the man who doesn't practice what he preaches. This is the fellow who talks the talk, but doesn't walk the walk. This is the "holier-than-thou" Christian who is blind to his own hypocrisy. The cure for this is to get in the Bible, to read it and to study it, and to get under the preaching of the word of God. People need to expose themselves to the Bible and allow God to shine the light of His truth on their lives. To walk in the light means to let God show you where you are wrong and where you need improvement, and then to apply the truth to your heart and life. It means to walk in obedience to the word of God. If one wants to enjoy God's blessings and maintain fellowship with Him, he is going to have to walk in the light.

The other phrase to take note of is found in 1 John 1, verse 9: "If we confess our sins." To stay in fellowship one must confess one's sins to God—not to the pastor, not to the priest, and not to the rabbi, but to God. The thing that breaks a believer's fellowship with God is sin. When a Christian disobeys the Lord and rebels against His commandments, the fellowship is broken. The child of God does not lose salvation, does not fall from grace, but becomes "at odds" with his heavenly Father. The Bible does not speak to the believer as it once did, church becomes a bore, and the Christian finds themselves "out of step" with other believers, and they do not enjoy the things of God like before. Simply put, Christians lose the joy of their salvation and find themselves backslidden.

From these two phrases, the reader can see there are two things that are key to maintaining fellowship with God—one must be careful not to live a lie, but to "walk in the light"; and one must be willing to come clean with God by confessing his sins to Him. If Christians will do these two things, the Bible says in 1 John 1:7 that "the blood of Jesus Christ, his [God's] Son, cleanseth us from all sin."

One of the most familiar hymns of the Christian faith is "Trust and Obey." Written by John H. Sammis in 1887, some of the words go like this:

> When we walk with the Lord in the light of His word,
> What a glory He sheds on our way!
> While we do His good will, He abides with us still,
> And with all who will trust and obey.
> Then in fellowship sweet we will sit at His feet,
> Or we'll walk by His side in the way;
> What He says we will do, where He leads we will go,
> Never fear, only trust and obey.
> Trust and obey, for there's no other way
> To be happy in Jesus, but to trust and obey.

*Relationship* is established by the new birth, which is experienced when a person by faith receives Christ as their own personal Savior. To get right with God as a non-Christian, a person must establish a relationship with God by being born again.

*Fellowship* is maintained by walking with Christ daily, which is experienced as a Christian reads the Bible, prays, lives right, and trusts God to meet daily needs. When one sins as a Christian, salvation is not lost— that issue was determined once and for all, for time and eternity, at the moment Christ was received as Savior, and an eternal relationship with God was established— but fellowship is broken and must be restored through the confession of one's sins to the Lord (1 John 1:9). To get right with God as a Christian, they must admit when they are doing wrong, and then confess those sins to God, and restore fellowship.

Years ago, a London newspaper held a contest. A prize would be given to whoever best answered this question: "Which is the shortest way to London?" Of the thousands of answers, the one that won the contest was this answer: "The shortest way to London is good company." If one has traveled much, the truth of this is easily understood.

Any trip seems shorter when there is good company. And the shortest way to heaven is to travel the road of life in the company of God's Son, Jesus Christ. If He is your traveling companion, the journey will be that much sweeter, the road that much easier, the trip that much more enjoyable, and the destination sure.

# SUMMARY

In this treatise, six biblical truths that provide evidence for the doctrine of eternal security have been presented. One chapter has been devoted to the related topic of the believer's assurance. "Once saved, always saved" is not a Baptist doctrine, per se, although it is Baptist doctrine—and, even more so, it is Bible doctrine. This is surely borne out by the teaching and testimony of Scripture.

The facts that have been considered—that Christians are saved by the grace of God, seated in heavenly places in Christ Jesus, sealed by the Holy Spirit, have undergone the divine surgery of the Lord, are sons in the family of God, and that the Scriptures attest to the eternal salvation of believers in Christ— are strong arguments for the Christian's eternal security.

## THE PRODIGAL SON: AN ILLUSTRATION OF THE ETERNAL SECURITY OF A BACKSLIDDEN BELIEVER

In the fifteenth chapter of the book of Luke is recorded what has been described as the best and most complete short story in the world: the account of the prodigal son. This story in the Bible is a vivid illustration of a backslidden, rebellious son of the

Father, who leaves home and wanders away from what he was taught and knew to be right. In the end, he "gets his heart right" and comes back to his father's house, where he is received back into fellowship, and there is rejoicing over the one sinner that repented.

In the account as recorded by Luke (15:11–24), the Lord Jesus says, "A certain man had two sons: And the younger of them said to his father, Father, give me the portion of goods that falleth to me. And he divided unto them his living." Notice that there were two brothers, and they had a mutual father. In the parable, the father typifies God the Father, and the sons represent the children of God.

"And not many days after the younger son gathered all together, and took his journey into a far country, and there wasted his substance with riotous living." The younger son got his things together and traveled far from home where he exhausted his inheritance in the pursuit of a sinful, unrestrained way of life. The term *prodigal* that is attached to this son comes from the verb *wasted* in this verse, which is a reference to his lifestyle of waste, abuse, and dissipation (i.e., the fact that he squandered his wealth until he had no more).

"And when he had spent all, there arose a mighty famine in that land; and he began to be in want." The young man spent all his substance, and then a great famine struck that damaged the economy, and he found himself in desperate straits. The word *want* means "need." So the Bible says that "he went and joined himself to a citizen of that country; and he sent him into his fields to feed swine." A devout Jew would want nothing to do with pig farming. The Law of Moses forbade the people of Israel from eating pork because the pig was considered an "unclean" animal, and it was not "kosher" meat (Leviticus 11:7). But this backslidden son of the father was in such desperation that he did something he would never before have thought to do.

"And he would fain [gladly] have filled his belly with the husks that the swine did eat: and no man gave unto him." He reached bottom and found himself in the depths of despair at this point in his life. Whereas he at first thought that the world would be his playpen, it quite literally became a pigpen when hard times came and he no longer had money or friends. It was at this point in his life that the Bible said: "And when he came to himself." This is the old rabbinical way of saying that he repented. In common vernacular, it means that the prodigal came to his senses.

And then "he said, How many hired servants of my father's have bread enough and to spare, and I perish with hunger! I will arise and go to my father, and will say unto him, Father, I have sinned against heaven, and before thee, And am no more worthy to be called thy son: make me as one of thy hired servants." This statement demonstrated his willingness to make things right with his father.

The next verse shows that, not only was he desirous to make reconciliation, but he followed through with his plan of action (what the theology books call *disposition*). "And he arose, and came to his father. But when he was yet a great way off, his father saw him, and had compassion, and ran, and fell on his neck, and kissed him. And the son said unto him, Father, I have sinned against heaven, and in thy sight, and am no more worthy to be called thy son."

The prodigal son repeated most of what he had rehearsed, but was unable to complete the refrain because his father was so overjoyed at his return that he interrupted him. "But the father said to his servants, Bring forth the best robe, and put it on him; and put a ring on his hand, and shoes on his feet: And bring hither the fatted calf, and kill it; and let us eat, and be merry: For this my son was dead, and is alive again; he was lost, and is found. And they began to be merry." Notice the son confessed that he had sinned and then expressed his feeling that he was no longer worthy to be called his father's son. But the father ignored his son's feelings, because his feelings did not change the fact that he was still the son of his father, and his father was still his father. The son and the father were related by blood and by birth, and nothing that the prodigal could do, would do, or did do, altered that fact.

The parable of the prodigal son is a wonderful story that illustrates the eternal security of the child of God. It is a beautiful picture of an errant child of God being reconciled to his heavenly Father after he sees the error of his ways and comes to his senses and repents and returns to the Lord. The prodigal returned home because he knew he could; he knew he was welcome back home; he knew that he was still loved and accepted by his father. (Even if he had doubts and fears about how his father would react, he still knew that his father would take him back.) The father never approved of what his son had done, but he accepted him back into fellowship once he repented and returned. God will restore fellowship with any of His wayward children who come back to Him, no matter how far they have roamed.

The doctrine of eternal security is a blessed doctrine that gives hope and assurance in a world of hopelessness and insecurity. No matter how far the prodigal may stray, he can always come back to the Father's house. The heavenly Father never approves of a

Christian's wandering and going astray, but He always accepts His born-again children back into fellowship when they repent of and confess their sins. (1 John 1:9)

Think back to Israel's deliverance from the fiery furnace of Egypt: If God did not deliver Israel from Egypt to destroy them in the wilderness (Exodus 16:3), then neither did He save His people from sin in this life to damn them to hell in the next life.

## A CLOSING THOUGHT AND APPEAL

If by chance there is one reading this who is not saved, and not sure of heaven, please consider some final thoughts. Salvation involves three things. They are the following:

1. The GIFT—eternal life. The Scripture is clear that "the *gift* of God is *eternal life* through Jesus Christ our Lord" (Romans 6:23). A gift is "something voluntarily transferred by one person to another without compensation."[60] In the Bible, the *something* is "eternal life," and it is *voluntarily transferred* by "God" to any and all repentant, believing sinners *without compensation*— that means "without money and without price" (Isaiah 55:1); God does not want anything in return for this gift, otherwise it would not be a gift. That is why the Bible says that salvation is by grace, apart from good works or human merit of any kind. If the gift were to be conditioned upon compensation, or be "taken back" for any reason, then the gift was not truly a gift. The fact that eternal life is a gift is evidence that salvation must be eternal.

2. The GIVER—God. The Bible says that "the gift of *God* is eternal life." The gift of eternal life is what God gives as the Giver. Maybe the most famous and familiar of all Bible verses, the beloved John 3:16, affirms that "God so loved the world, that he gave his only begotten Son, that whosoever believeth in him should not perish, but have everlasting life." When God gave His Son on Calvary to die for man's sins, Jesus paid the penalty for those sins, provided for mankind's salvation, and purchased the human race's redemption. In 1 John 5:11–12, it's plainly stated that eternal life, God's gift, is in God's Son, Jesus Christ, and that whoever has the Son, therefore, has eternal life. God would no more take back the gift of eternal life once given and received than He would take back the gift of His Son and the work that He did to accomplish mankind's redemption. The fact that *God gave* the gift of eternal life is more evidence that salvation must be eternal.

3. And the GIFTEE (receiver/recipient)—the believing sinner. Someone must be the recipient of the gift. That would be the believing sinner who receives Jesus Christ as personal Savior. Whoever receives the Son of God also receives the Gift of God, eternal life, because "this life is in his Son" (1 John 5:11).

For all those who have placed or will place their faith and trust in Jesus Christ for their soul's eternal salvation, they can *know* that they are saved and sure, safe and secure.

# APPENDIX 1

# BELIEVETH OR BELIEVED?

**N**ow, a point must be addressed that is made by those who deny eternal security when it comes to the definition of saving, keeping faith. Those who disagree with the teaching of eternal security argue that the faith that saves and keeps is a faith that "continues" believing. They teach that a Christian must maintain faith in order to maintain salvation. In other words, given the hypothetical case where a professing Christian was to stop believing and quit the faith, the proponents of Arminianism would say that that person "lost their salvation."

But the proponents of eternal security would say that such a professing Christian either (1) never was saved to begin with and therefore had no salvation to lose; that he was a professor but never a possessor, or that (2) no matter his practice, if that person had at one time placed their faith in Christ as personal Savior, that individual is still saved, and can never lose their salvation.

I, of course, agree with the latter, believing that Arminians misinterpret, misunderstand, and misapply the Biblical verses they use to press their case. The logical conclusion of their thinking leads to what sounds akin to nothing more or less than a works-based salvation. In their scheme of things, salvation depends on the Christian's continuance in the faith to stay saved; in their view, every lapse of faith or season of backsliding would result in losing one's salvation.

Among other arguments, Arminians base their case for conditional security (security based upon continued faith and continuous performance) on the verb tenses. One of their proponents, W. T. Purkiser, says, "The doctrine of eternal security makes the mistake of ignoring God's present tenses and changes them to the past tense."[61] In his opinion, the very verses used to prove eternal security actually deny it. For example, he quotes John 3:16 and says that "whosoever believeth" means whoever *is believing* in the present tense (i.e., to stay saved one must be *continually believing* in Christ in order to have eternal security). As he puts it: "More than initial faith is necessary.[62] ... Living by faith and continuing to believe are made the basis for final salvation.[63] ... Properly speaking, a believer is one who now believes, not one who may at some time in the past have believed. Believing is a process, a continued action."[64] He summarizes his position thus: "True security rests in the fact that saving faith is not a single historical act, but a present-tense, up-to-date, continuing process."[65]

To rebut this claim, Charles Stanley notes that although "those who subscribe to this argument understand the present tense to denote continuous, uninterrupted action,"[66] yet the "normal use of the present tense does not denote continuous, uninterrupted action."[67] According to his reasoning, in the real world of everyday life and conversation the present tense is used without being completely literal. Adapting from Dr. Stanley's excellent explanation, here are three examples that give support to this contention:

1. I have lived in Memphis, Tennessee, since 1986. For me to say that I live in Memphis does not mean that I am continuously within the city limits of Memphis. I can honestly say that I live in Memphis (present tense) in reference to my residence, and that would not be a false statement; however, if I were to leave the city for a period of time, it does not negate the fact that I live (present tense) in Memphis. Even if a person who claimed Memphis as their residence made frequent and regular trips out of town, say for business purposes or vacations, it would still be true that they lived (present tense) in Memphis. It can be said that such a person lives in, was living in, or lived in, Memphis, and all three expressions would mean the same thing: the person resides in Memphis, without having to be continually present in the city.

2. In John 4:14, when Jesus spoke to the woman at the well, He said to her about the water from Jacob's well that "whosoever drinketh of this water shall thirst again." The word *drink* is in the present tense, but if it be insisted upon that the tense be taken completely literal, the statement would literally mean that a person who was to drink continuously without interruption would thirst again. How could that be? Such an interpretation would be absurd, even contradictory. In light of this example, Stanley says "to interpret John's use of the present tense to mean continuous, uninterrupted believing is to make more out of the present tense than he intended."[68]

3. There are places where the word *believe* is used and translated as present tense in the English Bible, and the actual Greek tense is not present tense, but what is called

*aorist.* It is commonly agreed upon that the aorist tense is more indefinite, and that its focus is not so much on the *time* or the *continuation* of an event, but on the *fact* of that event. In Acts 16:31, the Bible says, "Believe on the Lord Jesus Christ, and thou shalt be saved." The word *believe* is translated as present tense in English, but the Greek tense is aorist. Why did Paul and Silas use the aorist and not the present tense to indicate continuous, uninterrupted believing, if that is what is required for salvation and security? Surely, the Holy Spirit could and would have led them to use the present tense in their instructions to the Philippian jailor to prevent any confusion; instead the Holy Spirit used the aorist tense, which weakens the argument that faith must be continuous and without interruption. The reason is that "the focus here is the *act* of his believing, not the maintenance of his faith or even his intention to maintain his faith."[69] Dr. Stanley summarizes: "God does not require a *constant attitude* of faith in order to be saved—only an *act* of faith."[70]

Ankerberg and Weldon in their book *How to Know You're Going to Heaven*[71] have this to say about the Greek tenses in regard to believing "in" or "on" Christ (e.g., John 3:16 and 3:36): "The participle construction of the present tense tells us that the believer is characterized" by a continuous believing, "but this cannot demand the loss of salvation should the believing theoretically cease believing. Those who believe Christians can lose their salvation and go to hell point out that the verb 'believe' is a present active participle" (and therefore means a Christian must continue to believe in order to be saved in the end).

They give three reasons why interpreting the Greek construction literally is a mistake:

The first reason they state is that the "Greek tenses never overturn established doctrine." In our current discussion, eternal security is counted as an established doctrine that cannot be overturned.

The second reason they give is the fact that a Christian is someone who is characterized by a continual trust in Christ for salvation anyway. Such faith is "hardly unexpected" for one who has been born again by the Spirit of God and is indwelt by the same Spirit.

And the third reason is that the idea of a necessary continuous faith is a "commonly held fallacy," in that "the Greek present tense does not demand a continuous nuance, but receives its aspect from the context and the nature of the action itself."

To conclude this appendix, the reader is referred back to chapter 2 and the argument from 2 Timothy 2:13 that "if we believe not, yet he abideth faithful: he cannot deny himself." It is clear from this scripture that our Savior will remain faithful to believers even in spite of a believer's faithlessness. So, what if a professing Christian *were* to stray from the Lord and even renounce his faith at some point in his life? Well, according to Paul's statement to Timothy, the Lord Jesus Christ will remain faithful! Certainly, this would be an extreme case, and maybe Paul is speaking in a hypothetical sense, to make the point that our salvation depends more on Christ's faithfulness than our faith [Galatians 2:16—we are "justified by the faith *of* Christ."]. To borrow from another Pauline statement: "For what if some did not believe? shall their unbelief make the faith of God without effect? God forbid." (Romans 3:3,4) Our initial faith in

Christ for salvation cannot be undone, even by our own lack of faith.

And let it be added, that in my personal experience, I've never met a truly born-again child of God who has ever renounced his faith.

## APPENDIX 2

# SHALL WE CONTINUE IN SIN, THAT GRACE MAY ABOUND?

L et us address the frequent criticism that the teaching of "once saved, always saved" becomes a license to sin and encourages believers to live a careless life.

Charles Finney comments concerning this and writes that "the greatest objection to the doctrine of justification by faith [and by extension, eternal security] has always been that it is inconsistent with good morals and opens the floodgates of iniquity. It has been argued that to maintain that men are saved by faith [and therefore be eternally secure] will make them disregard good morals and encourage them to live in sin, depending on Christ to justify them. Others maintain that the Gospel does in fact release men from obligation to obey the moral law so that a more lax morality is permitted under the Gospel than was allowed under the law." I agree with Mr. Finney when he clearly states in answer to these false charges that "justification by faith [with the accompanying blessing of eternal security] does not set aside the moral law, because the Gospel enforces obedience to the law and lays down the same standard of holiness. ... Justification by faith produces sanctification, or holiness, by producing the only true obedience to the law."[72] The Holy Spirit of God doesn't eradicate the Christian's sinful nature nor disable the Christian's ability to commit sin, but He does enable believers to live faithful, godly, and victorious lives for the glory of God.

The Bible asks and answers the question: "Do we then make void the law through faith? God forbid: yea, we establish the law" (Romans 3:31). The doctrine of justification by faith with its accompanying eternal security does not negate the law, or disrespect the law, but rather it "establishes" the law. It actually confirms the truth of the law and validates the law of God. The end of the law for righteousness is faith in Christ (Romans 10:4), and when one comes to faith in Christ for salvation, the law has accomplished its purpose, and "we establish the law."

In Romans 3:8, the apostle Paul, the Lord's theologian, says that those who preach the doctrine of salvation by grace and justification by faith are "slanderously reported" to say, "Let us do evil, that good may come." The idea is that if we are saved by grace, and that glorifies God, then why shouldn't we sin more so that God may be glorified more because then the grace of God could abound that much more, by covering more sins? As Paul put the question in Romans 3:5, "If our unrighteousness [sins] commend the righteousness of God [makes God 'look good'], *what shall we say?*" The apostle answers his own question as he furthers his argument and explanation in chapter six of Romans. He reasons in verses one and two: *"What shall we say then? Shall we continue in sin, that grace may abound? God forbid."* In other words, no, Christians should not continue to live in sin after their conversion to Christ. He goes on to say in verses 6 and 7: "Knowing this, that our old man is crucified with him, that the body of sin might be destroyed, that henceforth we should not serve sin. For he that is dead is freed from sin."

According to the Bible, we that are saved have been set free from the power of sin and should no longer serve sin. We are saved to serve the Lord Jesus Christ our Savior, not to live according to the flesh and commit sin with a cavalier attitude.

Again, do proponents of eternal security either directly or indirectly condone a sinful lifestyle for those who are saved, and saved forever? The answer is an emphatic "No, we do not." God forbid!

The moment we are saved the Holy Spirit enters into our bodies and sets up residence within us. At conversion, every Christian is made a "temple of God" (1 Corinthians 3:16), becomes a new creature in Christ (2 Corinthians 5:17), and receives a new nature (2 Peter 1:3, 4). The old desires to live sinfully are not replaced, but the Holy Spirit does place within God's people new desires to live a clean life and serve our Lord and Master. "Old things are passed away; behold, all things are become new." Many a preacher has said it this way: "When God saves us, He puts a new 'want to' in us. The sinful things we used to do we no longer want to do, and the spiritual things we didn't want to do before we now *want* to do."

To be direct and face the major objection to the teaching of eternal security, we will answer the most frequent and extreme question that people ask: "Can a person 'get saved' and then go out and rob a bank or kill someone, and still go to heaven?" The answer is yes! However, there are *consequences* to committing crime and committing sin.

In the world, the justice system will condemn a lawbreaker, and they will receive their just deserts. In the economy of heaven, the justice system of God's kingdom will not let sin by a believer go unpunished, either. In fact, if a Christian rebels against His Lord and Savior, he or she will suffer the consequences of their sin: the chastening of God in this life (Hebrews 12:5–11) and the future loss of rewards at the Judgement Seat of Christ (1 Corinthians 3:11–16; Romans 14:10b). The Bible is clear that a Christian will not be "condemned with the world" (go to hell), but that he will be "chastened of the Lord" (1 Corinthians 11:32; 3:17).

The writer of Psalm 89 speaks of the chastening in verses 30 to 34:

> If his children forsake my law, and walk not in my judgments; If they break my statutes, and keep not my commandments; Then will I visit their transgression with the rod, and their iniquity with stripes. *Nevertheless my lovingkindness will I not utterly take from him,* nor suffer my faithfulness to fail. My covenant will I not break, nor alter the thing that is gone out of my lips.

This passage shows us that when one of God's children becomes disobedient, the Lord will punish him with the rod and stripes (i.e., our heavenly Father will take a rebellious child out to the proverbial woodshed and give them a "whipping"). Now, we understand that this is not a literal, physical application of a rod with resulting stripes; however, God will get your attention when you get out of line. He may simply smite your heart with conviction, or if need be reach in and touch your health, your family, your finances, and so on, and you will know that God is not pleased. Every child of God has experienced chastening to some degree. The author of Psalm 119 was familiar with God's chastening. He wrote about God disciplining him in verses 71, 67, and 75:

- "It is good for me that I have been afflicted; that I might learn thy statutes." The Psalmist says the divine chastening was good for him, because it enabled him to learn the statutes of the Lord. (verse 71)
- "Before I was afflicted I went astray: but now have I kept thy word." Here, again, the Psalm writer tells us that God's chastening was instrumental in him learning to obey the word of God. There is nothing like a 'spanking' from the Lord to make you want to do right! (verse 67)
- "I know, O Lord, that thy judgments are right, and that thou in faithfulness hast afflicted me." The author of this Psalm credits the Lord with chastening him ("afflicting me") because of His faithfulness to the one He loved (Proverbs 3:11,12). And the child of God whose heart has been exercised by God's chastening readily admits that God's judgments, corrections, and statutes are right! (verse 75)

In the New Testament, Christians are admonished to not despise the Heavenly Father's chastening (Hebrews 12:5), because even though "no chastening for the present seemeth to be joyous, but grievous: nevertheless afterward it yieldeth the peaceable fruit of righteousness unto them which are exercised thereby" (Hebrews 12:11).

Let us close this section with an excerpt from Mr. Spurgeon's sermon based upon 1 John 2:1, "The Sinner's Advocate" (delivered at the Metropolitan Tabernacle in 1863):

The Apostle John presents us with a very clear and emphatic testimony to the doctrine of full and free forgiveness of sin. He declares that the blood of Jesus Christ, God's dear Son, cleanseth us from all sin, and that if any man sin, we have an Advocate. It is most evident that he is not afraid of doing mischief by stating this truth too broadly; on the contrary, he makes this statement with the view of promoting the sanctity of his "little children." The object of this bold declaration of the love of the Father to his sinning children is "that ye sin not." *This is a triumphant answer to that grossly untruthful objection which is so often urged by the adversaries of the gospel against the doctrines of free grace—that they lead men to licentiousness. It does not appear that the Apostle John so thought, for in order that these "little children" should not sin, he actually declares unto them the very doctrine which our opponents call licentious. Those men who think that God's grace, when fully, fairly, and plainly preached, will lead men into sin, know not what they say, nor whereof they affirm. It is neither according to nature nor to grace for men to find an argument for sin in the goodness of God.* Human nature is bad enough ... but even a natural conscience revolts at the baseness of sinning because grace abounds. Shall I hate God because he is kind to me? Shall I curse him because he blesses me? I venture to affirm that very few men reason thus. Man has found out many inventions, but such arguments are so transparently abominable that few consciences are so dead as to tolerate them. Bad as human nature is, it seldom turns the goodness of God into an argument for rebelling against him; as for souls renewed by grace, they never can be guilty of such infamy. The believer in Jesus reasons in quite another fashion. Is God so good?—then I will not grieve him. Is he so ready to forgive my transgressions?—then I will love him and offend no more ... Loved of God, we feel we must love him in return. Richly, yea, divinely forgiven, we feel that we cannot live any longer in sin. Since Jesus died to rid us from all uncleanness, we feel that we cannot crucify our Lord afresh, and put him to an open shame ... *And what if some men do pervert the doctrine?* Do not wicked minds corrupt everything? (Italics added)

# SALVATION AND ETERNAL SECURITY IN THE OLD TESTAMENT

In our study, we have dealt entirely with New Testament believers and their salvation and eternal security in Jesus Christ. While we have referenced some Old Testament verses to support our claim for New Testament eternal security, some may ask what about the Old Testament believers? Were they saved by faith? Did they actually have eternal security? Here are a few scriptural arguments that will hopefully provide a satisfactory explanation.

1.  There is not one example or case in the Old Testament where it can be proved that anyone ever actually "lost their salvation."

2.  If anyone in either the Old or New Testament "lost their salvation" then their salvation would have been a works-based salvation, and the Bible clearly teaches that salvation is not *of* works or *by* works. (Ephesians 2:8–9; Titus 3:5; Isaiah 64:6)

3. Of the examples given in the New Testament of Old Testament saints, we do not find any of them lost their salvation. Of those mentioned, three deserve our particular attention: Abraham, David, and Lot.

**ABRAHAM** is spoken of by the apostle Paul in his letter to the Romans (chapter 4:1–4) and by James in his epistle (chapter 2:20–24). Paul tells us that Abraham was justified by faith, and not by works, and that he received imputed righteousness as a result. He is set forth as an example of Old Testament salvation by faith *before* the dispensation of Law. In James, we see the outward evidence of Abraham's salvation, which was his works. His works proved that he had saving faith. Paul addresses the fact that Abraham was justified in the sense that God *declared* him righteous in a *legal* manner whereas James addresses the fact that Abraham was justified in the sense that he *demonstrated* that he had saving faith in a *behavioral* manner (his works showed he had the right kind of faith—see verses 18 and 24: "I will *shew* thee my faith by my works," and "Ye *see* then how that by works a man is justified.")

**LOT** is spoken of by the apostle Peter in his second epistle: in chapter 2, Lot is called just and righteous, and referred to as godly (verses 7, 8, 9). If you know the story of Lot, you know that there was no outward evidence of him being a saved man, and if there was a case of a man losing his salvation in the Old Testament, it could easily have been Lot. It is my contention that Lot was saved by faith and received imputed righteousness just like his uncle Abraham did. His conversion experience is not recorded in the Bible, but if he was just and righteous he had to have been a saved man who was justified by faith, even as Abraham was.

**DAVID** is spoken of by the apostle Paul in the book of Romans also (chapter 4:5–8), in the same context as Abraham. The difference is that David is typical of Old Testament salvation *during* the dispensation of Law. David was also justified by faith apart from works, and as a result he too received imputed righteousness. Again, if there was a person in the Old Testament who should have lost his salvation, it would have been David. He committed two sins for which there was no provision under the Law for forgiveness: adultery and murder. The penalty was death without mercy. Yet God forgave him, and he was allowed to live. Now, you must remember that the death penalty for an offender did not send him to hell but to the grave. The punishment was a civil penalty for a temporal crime. If a man broke the laws that David did, he would have been stoned to death, but that doesn't mean that he would go to hell. David was saved, justified and had righteousness imputed to him; his sins were not imputed to him (see Romans 4:6–8 and the original quote from Psalm 32:1–2). David was never in danger of losing his salvation; he may have *thought* he was (Psalm 51:12), but he wasn't.

4. The verses dealing with salvation by faith and eternal security that are found in the Gospels are Old Testament verses. The Gospels (Matthew, Mark, Luke, and John) are truly transitional books, and in them, the Bible is moving from the Old Testament to the New Testament. Remember that the New Testament actually begins when Jesus Christ dies on the Cross because a testament is not in force until the testator is dead (Hebrews 9:16–17). This means that almost all of the Gospels, except for the last few chapters of each, is actually still in the Old Testament dispensation, under the Law of Moses. Therefore, the verses and conversion accounts recorded during the life and ministry of Jesus Christ in the Gospels are Old Testament doctrine as taught by the Lord Jesus

Christ (and according to the apostle Paul, if a man does not consent to the words of Christ, he doesn't know what he is talking about [1 Timothy 6:3–5]).

Here are some things to consider when asking if an Old Testament believer can lose his salvation:

- An account of a sinner saved by faith before the Cross under the Old Testament dispensation of Law—In Luke 7:36–50, we have the story of a woman, who is a sinner, and comes to worship the Lord Jesus Christ. In the account, the Lord does not heal her of any disease, so this is not a "type" of salvation for anyone—it *is* salvation. Jesus plainly forgives her sins (verse 48) and clearly tells her that she is saved by faith (verse 50), and this happens while the Old Testament is still in effect.

- An Old Testament verse that teaches salvation by faith, accompanied by a promise of eternal security, to people who are living in the Old Testament dispensation of Law—In John 5:24, Jesus said, "Verily, verily, I say unto you, He that heareth my word, and believeth on him that sent me, hath everlasting life, and shall not come into condemnation; but is passed from death unto life." Here the Lord Jesus Christ says that *if* a person hears his word and believes on him that sent him, *then* that person has everlasting life and shall not come into condemnation, but is passed from death unto life. I believe that John 5:24 is the key to understanding the similarity between Old and New Testament salvation, and also the major difference.

The similarities between both Old and New Testament salvation are that salvation is by faith in God (believing on him that sent Christ: Jehovah the Creator and Redeemer—the God and Father of our Lord Jesus Christ), it requires a blood atonement (Leviticus 17:11; Hebrews 9:22— "without [the] shedding of blood, there is no remission [of sins]"), and it is accompanied by eternal security ("shall not come into condemnation"). The major difference is this: in the Old Testament no one knew the name of the Messiah; in the New Testament His name is revealed. That is why Jesus told the people that they needed to "believe on him that sent me" (i.e., God). That is what Old Testament saints did—they put their faith and trust in God for their salvation (Isaiah 45:22), looking forward to the coming Redeemer. But they did not know His name! In Proverbs 30:4 the Bible asks, "What is his name, and *what is his son's name*, if thou canst tell?" Well, they knew God by the name of Jehovah, but *they did not know His son's name*—but in the New Testament His name is revealed: Jesus Christ.

The famous American nineteenth-century evangelist Charles G. Finney said, "The whole sum and substance of revelation, like converging rays, all center on Jesus Christ and His divinity and atonement. All that the prophets and other writers of the Old Testament said about salvation comes to Him. The Old Testament and the New—all the types and shadows—point to Him. All the Old Testament saints were saved by faith in Him. Their faith terminated in the coming Messiah, as the faith of the New Testament saints did in the Messiah already come."[73]

The German reformer Martin Luther in his *Commentary on Galatians* seems to concur with this idea. He cites the case of Cornelius in the book of Acts where there he is called a "just man" (see 10:2, 22). Luther believed that Cornelius is called just in the same sense that Lot was called just and righteous in 2 Peter 2:7–8. He believed therefore that Cornelius was actually a saved man who was justified by God through faith. He states, "Cornelius was a just and holy man because of his faith in Christ who was to come. … If Cornelius had died before Christ was revealed, he would not have been damned, because he had the faith of the fathers, who were saved by faith only in Christ to come. He remained always a Gentile, uncircumcised and without law, and yet he worshiped the selfsame God, whom the fathers worshiped by faith in the Messiah to come. But now, because Messiah was already come, it was necessary that it should be shown to him by the Apostle Peter that he was not now to be looked for, but that He had already come."[74]

He goes on to say: "This teaching concerning Christ believed in before His coming, and in Christ come, is very necessary to be known. For seeing that Christ is now revealed, we cannot be saved by faith in Christ to come, but we must believe that He is already come, has fulfilled all things and abolished the law. Therefore it was necessary that Cornelius should be brought to another belief, not that Christ was yet to come, as he believed before, but that He was already come. So faith gives place to faith: 'from faith to faith' (Romans 1:17)."[75] When Peter recounts the evangelistic meeting at Cornelius' house and gives his mission report to the church in Judea, he relates that he was sent for to "tell [them] words, whereby [he] and all [his] house shall be saved" (Acts 11:14; cf. 10:6, 32–33). And Peter makes it clear that salvation was for those "who believed on the Lord Jesus Christ" (Acts 11:17).

Everyone is saved by the *merits* of the Cross. However, those in the Old Testament never actually heard or understood the *message* of the Cross. Only those in the New Testament have actually heard and been given the opportunity to believe the *message* of the Cross.

I believe this is one of the distinctions between Old and New Testament salvation. No one in the Old Testament was told to "believe on the Lord Jesus Christ," or to "receive" Christ as personal Savior. Not even the disciples who followed Jesus in His earthly ministry understood the Cross and its implications (see Luke 18:31–33).

It is only true theologically that those in the Old Testament "looked forward to the Cross." The believers in the Old Testament did not understand that Christ was going to die on the Cross (again, look to Luke 18:31–33). But in believing that Jesus was "the Christ," the Messiah of Israel, and the "Son of God" (John 11:27; Acts 8:37; 1 John 5:1), those under the Old Testament dispensation were saved by the *merits* of the Cross whose *message* they did not yet understand. The New Testament epistles, particularly of the apostle Paul, explained the death, burial, and resurrection of Jesus Christ, and those who had believed in Jesus as "the Christ," before the Cross, would after the Cross understand and acknowledge and accept the message of the Cross. (See the account of some 'stragglers' in Acts 19:1–5. They were disciples of John the Baptist who when they met Paul, accepted his message concerning salvation by believing on Christ.)

This is the unfolding of truth we call *progressive revelation*. The truth was there all the time, but not completely explained or understood. The old maxim is that the Old Testament is the New Testament concealed, and the New Testament is the Old Testament revealed.

In actuality, on this side of the Cross, we do look back to the Cross for our salvation, and are saved by the *merits* of the Cross by believing the *message*. The Old Testament saints were looking forward to the Cross in theory from our standpoint, and were saved by the *merits* of the Cross without actually knowing about it or understanding it; they simply had faith in what God told them and doing what God said do in the dispensation in which they lived. (This leads us into the teaching found in Hebrews 11:39–40)

So, in John 12:44, "Jesus cried and said, He that believeth on me, believeth not on me, but on him that sent me." In the New Testament (and in the transitional phases of the Gospels) a person "believe[s] on the Lord Jesus Christ" in order to be saved (Acts 16:31); and when a person believes on Christ for salvation, he has in essence believed on the One that sent Christ–God. And by the same token, in the Old Testament when a person put their faith in God to save them, they were in essence believing on the Lord Jesus Christ, without necessarily realizing that is what they were doing. So when Abraham and Lot and David put their faith in God and believed in the Lord for their salvation, they were actually putting their faith and trust in Jesus Christ! And if John 5:24 holds true, they received eternal security along with their salvation. (In this connection, see also Romans 4:24 and 1 Peter 1:21, and notice how the wording agrees with these statements and our comments: salvation is through faith in the true God of the Bible and what He did for us in regards to His Son dying for our sins and rising from the dead.)

I will end this section with a quote from the "Prince of Preachers," Charles Haddon Spurgeon, and a closing comment: "We do not find many of what we can accurately call conversions in the Old Testament. It is a record of a dim dispensation in which we rather see the types of things than the things themselves; but I should suppose that the priests, if they had been inspired to write what they often heard, would have been able to tell of many instances of deep conviction which would be made known in connection with the sin offerings and the trespass offerings, and they probably saw many instances of persons who henceforth led a new life and ceased from the sin which they had confessed over the victim's head. Of conviction, confession, and conversion they must have seen a great deal, but records we have none." (From the sermon "Manasseh") [76]

According to Spurgeon's quote, the Old Testament was a "dim dispensation" without records of clear-cut conversions; however, this is only true if you discount the Gospel conversion accounts, which are technically Old Testament. Even if we discount the Gospel records, it seems very clear that the way of salvation for the Old Testament saints was by grace alone, through faith alone, in Jehovah God and His Son, the Lord Jesus Christ. And, I would contend, based upon the overall teaching of Scripture, that individual Old Testament saints had eternal security.

# ENDNOTES

## Introduction

1 Ankerberg and Weldon, *How to Know You're Going To Heaven* (Eugene, Oregon: Harvest House Publishers, 2014), 23.

2 Charles Ryrie, *So Great Salvation* (Wheaton, Illinois: Victor Books, 1989), 137.

3 Lewis Sperry Chafer, *Salvation: God's Marvelous Work of Grace* (Grand Rapids, MI: Kregel Publications, 1991), 87.

4 New Advent, Catholic Encyclopedia Entry, http://www.newadvent.org/cathen/12403a.htm.

5 Fred Pascall MI, Internet Article: *The Deadly Sins of Presumption and Despair.* http://www.thedefender.org/THE%20DEADLY%20SINS%20OF%20PRESUMPTION%20AND%20DESPAIR.html.

6 W. T. Purkiser, *Security: The False and the True* (Kansas City, Missouri: Beacon Hill Press of Kansas City, 1956), 28.

7 Charles G. Finney, *Living for God* (New Kensington, Pennsylvania: Whitaker House, 1985), 217.

8 Dan Corner, *The Believer's Conditional Security: Eternal Security Refuted* (Washington, PA, Evangelical Outreach, 2000).

9 Charles Stanley, *Eternal Security: Can You Be Sure?* (Nashville: Thomas Nelson Publishers, 1990), 20.

10 John Maxwell, *Relationships 101: What Every Leader Needs to Know* (Nashville: Thomas Nelson Publishers, 2003), 9.

# Chapter 1

11  Lewis Sperry Chafer, *Grace: The Glorious Theme* (Grand Rapids: Zondervan Publishing House, 20th Printing January 1977), 78, 79.

12  Charles Spurgeon, *All of Grace* (Grand Rapids: Baker Book House, 1976), 113.

13  Chafer, 55.

14  Finney, 217, 219, 220, 223.

15  Spurgeon, 42.

16  Spurgeon, 60.

17  Spurgeon, 60–61.

18  Ryrie, 122.

19  E. M. Bounds, *The Weapon of Prayer* (New Kensington, Pennsylvania: Whitaker House, 1996), 40.

20  Bounds, 27.

21  Ryrie, 122.

22  Purkiser, 31–32.

23  Purkiser, 28.

# Chapter 2

24  J. D. Greear, *Stop Asking Jesus Into Your Heart* (Nashville: B&H Publishing Group, 2013), 43–45.

25  Edward T. Hiscox, *The Hiscox Standard Baptist Manual* (Valley Forge: Judson Press, 1965), 16.

26  Merriam-Webster Online Dictionary, http://mw1.merriam-webster.com/dictionary/body.

27  Watchmen Nee, *Sit, Walk, Stand* (Wheaton: Tyndale House Publishers, 1984), 20.

28  Nee, 20.

29  Nee, 21.

30  Nee, 21.

31  Ron Rhodes, *Reasoning From the Scriptures with Muslims*, (Eugene, OR: Harvest House Publishers, 2002), 253–254.

32  Dr. M.H. Tabb, *The Security of the Believer as Guaranteed by the Godhead* (Fort Walton Beach: Foundation Ministries, 1982), 20.

33  Nee, 17.

34  Hiscox, 17.

## Chapter 3

35  C. I. Scofield, *The Scofield Reference Bible*. (Oxford: Oxford Press, 1917), note 4, 1250.

36  Scofield, Note 1, 1328.

37  Stanley, 54.

38  Daniel 6:8; Esther 1:19.

39  Merriam-Webster Online Dictionary, http://mw1.merriam-webster.com/dictionary/earnest (Entry 3).

40  In the case of the Christian, the price was *fully paid* at Calvary, but the "purchased possession" will not be *claimed* until our Lord comes for His bride, the church, at the rapture. God has purchased the church, and the earnest of the Spirit is like a storage fee to secure the merchandise against resale while it remains in the devil's storehouse. The individual Christian will be claimed and removed at death, and the church as a whole at the rapture. (See Tabb, 27)

41  Comments on the Greek word, *tetelestai*, from a radio sermon by Hal Lindsey (date, sources unknown). Also see comments by Ankerberg and Weldon, 69–70.

42  Rhodes, 254.

## Chapter 4

43  David Cloud, Internet Article: *"What Do You Think about Peter Ruckman?"* Fundamental Baptist Information Services.

44  Constance B. Reid, "Love Found A Way."

## Chapter 5

45  John R. Rice, *Can a Saved Person Ever Be Lost?* (Murfreesboro, Tennessee: Sword of the Lord Publishers, n.d.) 16.

46  H. A. Ironside, *The Eternal Security of the Believer* (New York: Loizeaux Bros., 1934) 6.

47  Scofield, note 2, 1250.

48  William Evans, *The Great Doctrines of the Bible* (Chicago: Moody Press, 1912, [1976 Printing]) 161.

49  Evans, 161–162.

50  Evans, 162.

51  Evans, 163.

52  Internet Article: "What Does It Mean That Christians Are Adopted By God?," posted on gotquestions.org — https://www. gotquestions.org/ Christian-adoption.html

53  Evans, 163.

## Chapter 6

54  Arthur W. Pink, *Gleanings In Genesis* (Chicago: Moody Press, 1922, 1950, [Fifteenth Printing, 1978]) 287–288.

## Chapter 7

55  Ryrie, 137.

56  Ryrie, 142.

57  Paul Lee Tan, *Encyclopedia of 7,700 Illustrations: Signs of the Times* (Rockville, Maryland: Assurance Publishers, 1979, [1982 Printing]) 1192.

58  Internet Article, posted on *HarbourLights.com* website— http://www. harbourlights.com/catalog/2003/hl_gold_bridge.htm.

## Summary

59  Words and music by Johnny Cash, 1958.

## Appendix 1

60  Merriam-Webster Online Dictionary, http://mw1.merriam-webster. com/dictionary/gift
    Also see internet link http://legal-dictionary.thefreedictionary.com/gift for the following information about the legal definition of "gift."

*A voluntary transfer of property or of a property interest from one individual to another, made gratuitously to the recipient. The individual who makes the gift is known as the donor, and the individual to whom the gift is made is called the donee.*

GIFT, conveyancing. A voluntary conveyance; that is, a conveyance not founded on the consideration of money or blood. The word denotes rather the motive of the conveyance; so that a feoffment or grant may be called a gift when gratuitous. A gift is of the same nature as a settlement; neither denotes a form of assurance, but the nature of the transaction. Watk. Prin. 199, by Preston. The operative words of this conveyance are do or dedi. The maker of this instrument is called the donor, and he to whom it is made, the donee. 2 B. Com. 316 Litt. 69; Touchs. ch. 11.

GIFT, contracts. The act by which the owner of a thing, voluntarily transfers the title and possession of the same, from himself to another person who accepts it, without any consideration. It differs from a grant, sale, or barter in this, that in each of these cases there must be a consideration, and a gift, as the definition states, must be without consideration.

2. The manner of making the gift may be in writing, or verbally, and, as far as personal chattels are concerned, they are equally binding. Perk. Sec. 57; 2 Bl. Com. 441. But real estate must be transferred by deed.

3. There must be a transfer made with an intention of passing the title, and delivering the possession of the thing given, and it must be accepted by the donee. 1 Madd. Ch. R. 176, Am. ed. p. 104; sed vide 2 Barn. & Ald. 551; Noy's Rep. 67.

4. The transfer must be without consideration, for if there be the least consideration, it will change the contract into a sale or barter, if possession be delivered; or if not, into an executory contract. 2 Bl. Com. 440.

5. Gifts are divided into gifts inter vivos, and gifts causa mortis; and also' into simple or proper gifts; that is, such as are to take immediate effect, without any condition; and qualified or improper gifts, or such as derive their force upon the happening, of some condition or contingency; as, for example, a donatio causa mortis. Vide Donatio causa mortis; Gifts inter vivos; and Vin. Ab. h. t.; Com. Dig. Biens, D 2, and Grant; Bac. Ab. Grant; 14 Vin. Ab. 19 3 M. & S. 7 5 Taunt. 212 1 Miles, R. 109.

A Law Dictionary, Adapted to the Constitution and Laws of the United States. By John Bouvier. Published 1856.

61  Purkiser, 28.
62  Purkiser, 30.
63  Purkiser, 32.
64  Purkiser, 28.
65  Purkiser, 32–33.
66  Stanley, 83.
67  Stanley, 84.
68  Stanley, 86.
69  Stanley, 87.
70  Stanley, 80.

## Appendix 2

71  Ankerberg and Weldon, 134.
72  Finney, 228–229.

## Appendix 3

73  Finney, 222
74  Martin Luther, Commentary on Galatians (Grand Rapids: Fleming H. Revell, 1924, 1988 [Paperback edition, 2nd Printing, 1999] 133–134.
75  Luther, 134.
76  C. H. Spurgeon, Seven Wonders of Grace (Grand Rapids: Baker Book House, 1978 [2nd Printing, 1979]) 9.

Printed in the United States
by Baker & Taylor Publisher Services